# Man's Dominion

# Man's Dominion

*Our Violation of the Animal World*

MONICA HUTCHINGS
and
MAVIS CAVER

Rupert Hart-Davis London 1970

First printed in Great Britain 1970

Rupert Hart-Davis Ltd
3 Upper James Street
Golden Square
London W1R 4BP

ISBN  0  246  63990  3

Printed in Great Britain by
Ebenezer Baylis and Son Ltd
The Trinity Press, Worcester, and London

# Contents

# List of Illustrations

*Authors' Note*

The authors offer their grateful thanks and acknowledgment for help and co-operation and also for permission to quote to:

Mr Arthur Brisco, The National Equine Defence League
Major K. C. Priestley of the RSPCA
Mr Roy Mark Pattison, Anglo East European Fund for Animal Welfare
Capt. MacMichael & Mr H. Warner, Performing Animals Defence League
Miss Kathleen Mitchell, Appeals Secretary, RSPCA, Bath
Mrs Barbara Macdonald, Dartmoor Livestock Protection Society
Mrs Ruth Murray, Point Nature Reserve
Mrs J. Westren, New Forest Society
Lady Dowding, Beauty Without Cruelty
Rev. Michael Fryer, Crusade Against All Animal Cruelty
Mrs H. Willoughby Dewar, Council Against Bullfighting
Mrs Ruth Harrison, Advisory Committee Factory Farming
Miss Irene Heaton, Captive Animals Protection Society
Mr S. Rowley, The League Against Cruel Sports
Mr S. Pepper, National Society for Abolition of Cruel Sports
Nina Warner Hooke for material on seals and sealing
Mrs Avril Dalby for material on horse management and show jumping
Mr Harvey Metcalf, Scottish Society for the Prevention of Vivisection
Mrs Gretchen Boland, Rochester, USA
Dr Desmond Morris
UFAW
Ferne Animal Sanctuary, Dorset
The Canadian Wild Horse Society
Mr B. G. Atkinson, Australia
Mr Patrick Moore, FRAS
Canon Edward Carpenter
F. Howard Lancum
Leslie G. Pine

Miss G. Barter
Dr Ernest Neal
Brian Davies, New Brunswick Society for the Prevention of Cruelty to
    Animals
Mrs K. Taylor Smith, the Brooke Hospital for Animals, Cairo
Mrs Hosali, Society for the Protection of Animals in North Africa
Philip Knightly
Mr Robert Morris, MRCVS
F. Fraser Darling, DSc, PhD, LLD, FIBiol, FRSE
Professor Dudley Stamp, CBE
Glenda Spooner, Chairman, Ponies of Britain
Mr John Pitt, BUAV
Mrs Vera Ryder
Mrs Jean Pyke
Mrs Vera Sheppherd
Mr Eric Ashby
E. A. Batty, ALA
Capt. Robert Shorediche Churchward
Mr Peter Scott
Rev. R. Fuller, Exmoor vicarage

# Introduction

When Robert Burns turned up the nest of a field mouse with his plough share, John Blane, the farm-servant who had a *pettle* or plough-cleaning utensil in his hand, made an attempt to kill the escaping creature. Burns checked him, asking what ill the mouse had ever done him.

That evening the poet read out the verse which had been inspired by this incident:

> I'm truly sorry man's dominion
> Has broken nature's social union,
> And justifies that ill opinion
> Which makes thee startle
> At me, thy poor earthborn companion
> And fellow mortal.

Burns did not lack compassion, a ready impulse to save, although he lived during an age that was notorious for inhumanity to both man and beast. Two centuries later, in spite of a few advances, the animal kingdom generally would be all too justified in holding the same 'ill opinion' of man's dominion over other forms of life.

Our own age has seen such mass destruction of human life, such violence and suffering that it becomes increasingly difficult to obtain serious consideration for the brute creation without being accused of faulty priorities. Yet, as Lamartine points out, 'The difference between cruelty to man and cruelty to animals is one of degree only, not of kind. If we include animals in the law of duty and compassion, as we are commanded to, we work at the same time for the uplifting of our fellow-men.' Reform comes gradually, but whatever charges of 'crank' and 'sentimentalist' may be levelled at the would-be reformer it is most certainly better to have lit one small candle than to have sat cursing the darkness.

The obloquy of such a label inhibits 'interference' when we witness cruelty or neglect. Yet perhaps more danger lies in the opposite direction. During the course of a St Francis day sermon in Coventry Cathedral in 1964, the Rev. A. D. Belden, BD, DD, FPhS, pointed out:

> There is no more widespread and foolish fallacy afflicting human judgement today than the idea that Man's tender emotions can be despised and discarded in favour of his hard and tough emotions. We are stupidly afraid of being sentimental in these days, but apparently not so fearful of being brutalised . . . if in our medical services, in our industries and commerce, sport and leisure, an ever vaster number of our citizens have got to harden their hearts against animal suffering, they will be but a hair's breadth from equal cruelty to mankind. All who exercise cruelty upon animals, especially those who do it habitually as a routine of research or of sport, should be warned of the moral damage they do to themselves. No man can systematically kill compassion in his heart and remain what he was. No human vice or virtue can be departmentalised. It at last corrupts, or glorifies, the whole.

Shakespeare was very certain of the power of compassion to elevate man to his proper status above the beast, most succinctly expressed in these lines from *Titus Andronicus*:

> Wilt thou draw near the nature of the Gods?
> Draw near them then in being merciful;
> Sweet mercy is nobility's true badge.

But to show mercy to one kind of life and implacable brutality towards another, in fact to try and departmentalize such fundamental instincts as the will to save or destroy, may lead to the kind of moral climate which made Belsen and Buchenwald possible. To lack the impulse of mercy towards those of the animal kingdom which are in our power sets us on the road towards indifference to the suffering and terror of those of our own species who are in our power.

Opposition to animal welfare suggests that animals are preferred to children as objects of our compassion, but contrary to widely held belief, there are many more charities and appeals concerned with children. The Annual Charities Digest is largely filled with organizations dealing with children. These run to thirty-five pages of print, while those dealing with animals in all their forms take up four pages. The Spastics Society raised over three million pounds in one year. Dr Barnardo's Society claims over three million and the Church of England

Children's Society counts on over a million annually. The general fund of the National Society for the Prevention of Cruelty to Children is six million pounds and over three hundred million pounds is allotted by the Government on child welfare each year (not counting education). These figures make nonsense of the gibe that the RSPCA has all the nation's bequests and that we care more about animals than children.

Twentieth-century man must pose many questions regarding his attitudes to animal life. He will probably claim to be more humane, since it is axiomatic to proclaim that ignorance breeds cruelty. But the modern world displays cruelty of an equal degree springing from venality and greed and the demand for a constantly 'higher' standard of living. In the name of progress, anything goes. And man must ask himself if his apparent mastery over his environment is not divorcing him for ever from the source of his own life.

That the evidence collated in this book cannot be classified as pleasant, the authors are only too well aware. The great enemies of progress and reform are complacency and ignorance, but we believe with Thomas Hardy:

If way to the better there be, it exacts a full look at the worst.

# Performing Animals

'Fools were made for showmen to deceive'
P. J. BARNUM

From time immemorial man has trained animals not only to work for him and hunt for him, but to entertain him. The subduing and training of ferocious wild beasts to do his exact bidding represented a formidable victory over the wild, and helped to reinforce his claim to the title of 'Lord of Creation'. Given the weapons, anyone can kill an animal, but not anyone can coerce jungle beasts into performing complicated tricks often completely alien to natural instincts. It was, and still is, this show of mastery on the part of a relatively puny animal that has made the circus such a popular spectacle.

The mystique of the sawdust ring and the Big Top has further been enhanced by the view of it taken by such artists as Degas, Lautrec, Dame Laura Knight and Picasso and members of the Cirque Medrano in Paris. Their idealized clowns, spangled bareback riders and tinselled performers have helped to create a world apart and unchanging, while other standards of glamour are forever altering. Yet we have found from personal experience that once the question of performing animals and their capture, breaking and training methods are really examined it is impossible to view them with equanimity. Leading humane organizations share this view.

From time to time the National press carries advertisements for the work of the RSPCA. One series has dealt entirely with circus animals. Under pictures of a lion jumping through a flaming hoop, and an elephant balancing his immense weight on one foot upon an upturned tub, comes the statement:

> Because of the severity of training and discipline necessary in per-
> formances to a time-table and of the misery inherent in travel and in

close confinement, the RSPCA opposes by all the means in its power exhibitions or presentations of performing animals of any kind.

Hard words? Sweeping statements? If you think so, why has no large circus company sued the Society for misrepresentation, for defamation of character, for publishing a libel? Instead the great circus proprietors prefer to go their own way, largely ignoring criticism and opposition, although one of their number has gone on record as cynically declaring that 'fools are made for showmen to deceive'.

At school in London we lived very close to the south gate of the Zoo. Always having a deep interest in animals, wild or tame, we spent a great deal of time in the Zoological Gardens and came to know the inmates very well. In those days only members were allowed in on Sundays, and many a Sunday we roamed the Zoo from end to end studying the accommodation, methods of feeding, and the behaviour of the animals. Some of the captives (such as the sea-lions) seemed very content, others were plainly dragging out lives of extreme misery or at least of boredom in what amounted to a life sentence of close confinement. Yet they were well looked after, adequately fed, and most, in addition to their sleeping and living quarters, had some kind of outside run or enclosure.

When we saw our first circus, with the usual attendant menagerie of animals that could be seen for an extra sixpence, we realized that the animals of the London Zoo were living in relative freedom.

We can still remember the solitary ape in what amounted to a tiny box, like an upright coffin, a leopard that so filled his cage that one paw and tail protruded through the bars, and a mangy old lion with no room to turn round. These animals had not appeared in the ring, they were just on show, and presumably spent their entire lives in this kind of way, shunted from fair to fair like so much live (or half-alive) luggage.

For many years we did not go near the circus again, and then a few years ago came a semi-official assignment to visit the winter training quarters of a large tented circus. During the intervening years we had as farmers become even more interested in animal welfare but certainly not sentimental about animals themselves. If we had thought about the circus at all, we had assumed that conditions had improved, that the public opinion of childhood which tolerated the state of affairs, so well remembered, would have moved a few steps forward, and matters like performing animal training would safely be left to accredited welfare societies such as the RSPCA. We had a great deal to learn.

These winter quarters were spacious and well-run, the feeding and grooming of the animals eminently efficient. An outsider on a quick tour of the premises might gather but one impression, that the livestock were in good condition.

On the whole this is true of most of the surviving circuses in Britain today, though probably not so true of some smaller ones on the Continent. These animals are stock-in-trade, some of them are not easily replaceable, their value is immense. It would be folly to expect other than adequate feeding and maintenance. We saw no sick animals. Untrainable animals, those that fall by the way, are sold for what they will fetch to private zoos, collections or pet shops. Others are hired out to film and television companies, often with a handler attached; these animals are big business. What remains at winter breaking and training quarters, on the whole, is the cream of the performing animal world. They have passed the test, many have been broken at their place of capture (this is particularly true of the elephants) or partly trained with some Continental circus, where our laws do not apply.

We were taken all round these winter quarters on several occasions and also witnessed many acts being rehearsed in the ring. One was new, a tiger in a kind of howdah riding on an elephant's back. This was a 'first time ever' act, later to be equalled by the Moscow State Circus with a lion riding horseback, which in Paris in 1965 resulted in a horse being badly savaged and a good deal of criticism in the press about these unnatural combinations of 'natural enemies'.

Watching the tiger and elephant going through their act we received the impression that both animals loathed the whole proceeding, and were acting under considerable duress. In fact this act was fairly short-lived, as on the death of this particularly trainable tiger, no suitable replacement was found.

One of the lessons learned from this first visit inside what is, to the general public, forbidden territory, was that each circus has to compete with the others. This is the way to draw the crowds, to pull in the money, to clinch the television contracts. This means that more and more difficult acts have to be thought up and perfected, until some of them would seem to verge on the impossible.

Another lesson learned almost at once was that the inspectors of the RSPCA have no right in *training*-quarters on private land at all, unless specifically invited (in which case they see exactly as much as it is convenient for the showmen to let them see).

The topic was introduced over luncheon in the proprietors' wagon. We were discussing horses, having noticed how the 'Liberty' Palominos had tremendous knotted muscles to their rear quarters, gained through hours of walking and 'waltzing' on their hind legs only. This muscular development amounted almost to deformity.

Quite casually we threw out the question 'Do you ever have any trouble with the RSPCA?' They laughed and appeared to enjoy the joke hugely. 'I should say not' was the gist of their reply. 'The last chap of theirs who came poking his nose in here was very quickly seen off, and we haven't had any trouble with them since.'

We afterwards substantiated this story. Unless an inspector has been specifically called in to investigate some complaint, he has no right at all and is technically trespassing. The only people who are in any position to witness cruelty and make any such complaints are the employees of the circus itself, and as they are unlikely to jeopardize their bread and butter, winter quarters are in fact safe from any outside interference.

One of the defences put up by circus personnel when this topic is raised is that secrecy is absolutely necessary to the breaking in and training of new acts, as competition between circuses is keen. This is true and understandable, but it also affords the most perfect smoke-screen for what goes on when the circus is off the road, in winter breaking and training quarters.

By the time the tenting season begins, the general public sees only the finished act, all mistakes ironed out. Punishments are hardly necessary, the sight of whip or goad, the tone of voice, the gesture, are enough to remind the animal of what went on during the months of attrition when the man established the power of life and death over it and forever taught it who was master.

When the general public or the RSPCA are invited to witness training, they are not in fact being invited or permitted to see more than a *rehearsal*. All the gruelling hard work has been completed long before, well out of sight and sound of critical eyes and ears. The scars have had time to heal, a relationship between trainer or handler and the animal performer has been established. Very occasionally things go wrong, someone makes a mistake, there are minor incidents, but usually the whole finished act is foolproof, the animal concerned has become conditioned into something like an automaton. He has to, because unlike a pet dog, he cannot have any off days, cannot afford to defy his owner or suffer any lapses. The show must go on, and to time; and in the circus, timing is a matter of split seconds. The animal who makes the slightest mistake must be taught the hard way that nothing but perfect timing and obedience will do. The penalties for failure have to be so severe that the performer is unlikely to forget or commit the same mistake twice. And it must be remembered that animals in close captivity can be off-colour. But there are no understudies, and the show must go on.

This is particularly true of the *rosinbacks*, those broadbacked horses, keeping their steady pace round and round the confines of the ring, never putting a foot wrong, head secured in the small curving arch by a system of bearing or Newcastle running reins secured to the bit. One slight deviation, and the acrobatic pyramid on their backs would be endangered, maybe fatally injured. The rosinback learns early that he must not make the slightest mistake.

In the same way, Liberty horses are in fact anything but at liberty. The time-honoured phrase is a misnomer. Next time you see a picture of horses *At Liberty* (and the *Radio Times* is always showing pictures of circus acts, the great Bank Holiday standby) you will see that the position of the head is virtually 'in irons'. Reins from either side of the mouth run back to a martingale, while the plumed headdress often conceals the joins of other harness which ensures that the head is held in a rigid arch which looks spirited and mettlesome, but which we are assured by those who work with horses is unnatural and uncomfortable. Horses of this type are left many hours with their heads so secured. Yet the bearing rein for carriage horses was outlawed early this century.

Many people who do not particularly approve of circuses and who have reservations with regard to training methods will often declare that 'at least the horses enjoy it, such splendid animals!' If they could see some of the gadgets necessary to train a horse to waltz, change step, bow, laugh, etc., they might have second thoughts on this.

Trainers in their memoirs have been extremely frank over methods employed in obtaining the finished results with equine acts, apparently seeing no evil in the tricks of their trade. But experts outside performing animal circles have also published material on training methods. The following extracts from *Illustrated Horsebreaking*, by Captain M. H. Haynes, MRCVS, are of interest to those who think that the horses obviously enjoy it.

### Rearing and Walking on the hind legs
In a Circus a horse is taught to rear by taking the snaffle reins over his head and jerking them, so as to hurt his mouth, and by touching him with the whip in front. In a short time the horse will stand on his hind legs and walk about in obedience to the owner flourishing the whip. They are also taught to rear by bashing them under the jaw with a stock whip—such performances offend the principle of true horsemanship as they are stupid to look at.

*Laughing*

This meaningless trick is accomplished in the same way as a horse is taught to shake his head, by pricking him with a pin, but in this case the irritation is applied to the muzzle. The horse then learns on the signal being given to turn up his upper lip and show his teeth.

*Polka, Dancing etc.*

A circus horse 'At Liberty' is said to dance the polka when he changes the leg at every stride at the canter. The movement which is particularly difficult to teach may be obtained by the use of a long whip in getting the required changes of leg.

*Circling steadily at Liberty*

After having taught the horse to circle with the long reins, his head may be fixed in position with the side reins, with a leading rein attached to a cavesson. When you want to make him halt you should jerk the leading rein so as to make the noseband of the cavesson strike his nose and at the same time bring the point of the lunging whip in front of the face. By diminishing the painful action of the cavesson and by continuing the threatening use of the whip in front of the animal we shall be able to make him halt, run back or turn, by the whip alone.

The backward and upward tension exerted by the bearing rein, besides causing the neck to arch at a painful and unnatural angle, often forces the lower jaw down and the mouth wide open. This adds to the 'fiery steed' appearance so beloved by circus audiences, but at considerable cost to the animal. In November 1933 a trainer with Bertram Mills' circus was criticized by the Performing Animals' Defence League for cruel use of the bearing rein. In the *Radio Times* during March 1967 a picture of horses in Billy Smart's circus television show indicated use of the bearing rein and the same forced-open jaws. Conditions have not improved at all in the last thirty years.

Having witnessed the riot of the chimps' tea-party at the Zoo, we brought up this topic to our circus hosts. The reply was surprising. We were told that the training of chimps 'has to be harsh'. The use of the word *harsh* was very significant, coming from a trainer. We were told that chimps, for all their small size, are immensely strong and muscular. There is no cage for them and no distance between them and the presenters. They must be taught early that the man is absolute master. If they wear clothes, which most of them do and which they begin by disliking and fighting off, then only the harshest discipline and punishment will bring them to the point of submission and perfect obedience. And what of the arms round the neck and the grins of affection? We were told that the former is rather akin to the fawning of a dog – an 'I-have-done-what-you-wanted-so-don't-chastise-me' attitude. Desmond Morris, in a recent television programme on animal behaviour, made it clear that the chimpanzee's smile is more likely to be a grimace of anxiety and stress.

So we are deceived because we want to be deceived. The circus audience wishes to think that the human-like monkey, the little chimp in children's clothes, is enjoying it too and that it is all great fun. If you watch a chimp act closely you will see that there is a fair amount of violent hustle going on. Claw-like hands are snatched and placed elsewhere, a tug here, a push there keep the simian puppets going through their paces. Some of the acts are complicated and difficult. The Zoo tea-parties, on the other hand, were extempore, no exact timing, no hustle. The animals were left to please themselves and in doing so pleased the onlookers. To compare the two performances is no valid defence of chimpanzee training methods.

The old argument by pro-circus people or those who are ignorant of training methods, that animals love to perform tricks, is particularly feeble when compared with the kind of acts that circus dogs are compelled to do, or the complete lack of freedom they experience apart from their twice nightly appearance in the ring.

Naomi Jacob, who appeared at a theatre where there was a dog act, wrote, 'the dogs are in small pens or boxes, let out only to do their act at night. Bitches are most often used, as they will not foul their box if possible. When pens are opened they just could not wait to relieve themselves after such long cramped confinement, which obviously caused them much discomfort.'

A Hull theatre manager complained to the Performing Animals Defence League that three performing dogs were put in hutches three feet by two feet for twenty-three hours a day. Two had fits but were made to perform just the same. In 1944 the same League received a letter from one of the staff of a leading London music hall. 'Many members of the staff have seen the brutal treatment of these poor creatures. One is lame, another nearly blind. We have heard them yelp. These fourteen performing dogs get half a pound of meat between them every other day. They are looked after by a drunken man who yesterday burned it so they had none.' This referred to an act known as Cavalini's Dogs.

The back-somersault trick, a notoriously difficult act (which pro-circus people would have us think compares favourably with teaching a pet to sit up and beg) may result in the crippling or death of many animals before one can be induced to perform it correctly. Witnesses have described how Boxer dogs in striped jerseys performed in a football match act. One dog made a mistake and he was afterward thrashed until he was a cowering wreck in full sight of the others – as an example of what happens if the trainer is not obeyed implicitly.

But all this brutality is largely because children allegedly love to see the circus. It has recently been suggested that adults sublimate their own fantasies through their children. How many parents or grandparents going to the circus for the children's sake are in reality indulging their own tastes for noise, violence and unsophisticated laughs, or are reliving their own childhood when the circus was sometimes the only organized entertainment for the young, before the days of films and television? In our experience, children often seem quite blasé about visits to the circus and do not show the enthusiasm expected of them by their elders. Yet these same children will absorb 'wild life' programmes on television such as *Daktari* which are popular both in Britain and the States. And here it is interesting to note that the large animal training concern who provide the 'stars' for this type of production and who style themselves Africa USA have gone on record as stating that they refuse to employ circus trainers. The directors have stated that they insist on love and affection towards all their animals and that this is not compatible with circus methods!

There is a tradition that normal, nice children must love the circus, yet it is probable that they would miss the animal side of this entertainment less than adults wish to believe. Acrobats and clowns can be seen live and appreciated better in this medium than perhaps any other. Balancing feats, skill on the aerial trapeze, gravity-defying acts can all enlarge a child's awareness and understanding of the possibilities of the human body. But a child will learn little about the nature of a lion which jumps through a flaming hoop, not even perhaps that it has been forced to overcome its fear of fire, the natural enemy, by its omnipotent trainer. If children take their cue from grown-up behaviour, it is certainly not the healthiest kind of entertainment that encourages exploitation and violence of captive animals in this way.

Today, with transport more than ever streamlined and the accent on mobility, travelling cages, which all too often are also living quarters, are as cramped and as inadequate as ever. The great bears, both polar and brown, especially suffer from close confinement, sometimes spending their entire lives as showpieces without even the limited exercise afforded by appearances in the ring. And to those who have never actually been in a circus ring, its smallness may come as something of a surprise. The size has to be a uniform 42 feet in diameter, because acts are circulated internationally.

Bears, with their clumsy bulk and often grotesque carriage, have long been a victim of the travelling showman. The dancing bears of the Middle Ages and the chained travelling exhibits popular throughout Europe and Asia were with us well into this century and have not entirely disappeared from some remote areas. Because of their size and apparent fierceness, such animals were wonderful object lessons to illustrate man's dominion over the beasts.

The training of dancing bears used to consist of their being rigidly chained and forced to walk on hot coals, which made them lift their feet smartly to lessen the pain of burning. Nowadays instead of the coals there are electric hot-plates and goads, but the initial methods are essentially the same as ever. Bears have limited intelligence and are correspondingly hard to train to do anything complicated. This has always presented a challenge to the trainers and promoters who want to go one better. Only complete domination will result in a bear riding a bicycle or performing any of those futile and senseless tricks one may witness in present-day circus acts.

Russian trainers are foremost in producing performing bears. A. Maiorov of the Moscow State Circus has achieved fame with his bears' ice-hockey match. The Art Festival booklet brought out by the Ministry of Culture for the USSR in 1968 describes this act as 'not just a great accomplishment for the young animal trainer, but actually opens new vistas in animal training'.

Valentin Filatov with his bear circus is a great favourite in the USSR, to such an extent that his famous motor-cycling bear who rides a fully-powered machine round the ring at speed is featured on matchboxes and other small souvenir articles, rather as the *corrida* bull is in Spain. In the 1968 Art Festival book there is a glossy illustration of Filatov with a bear on either side of him, the three heads close together, and the anthropomorphic caption 'In the midst of a serious discussion with his charges'. The bears are not muzzled in the normal way where they can open their mouths slightly inside the framework. In this picture they have their jaws tightly bound by a broad band secured by another running up the head between the ears. Obviously their jaws are clamped securely together above the nostrils and no movement of any sort is possible.

When the Moscow State Circus visited Britain in the nineteen-sixties, one of their acts was a kind of carousel with bears strapped to it by headbands, being swung round like 'chairoplanes' at a fun fair. This particular act did not meet with universal approval and the British Press published much criticism, particularly after Peter Black of the *Daily Mail* asked, 'How did Gosha the wonder bear come by those deep lines across the top of his head and one down the side?' He had seen ominous marks on the bear's skin which looked like burns. The Circus went back to Russia, and the outcry died a natural death.

Short of making an international incident of the affair, perhaps there was little to be done in this case, but RSPCA inspectors have been known to express disquiet over acts involving performing bears. One commented after an actual performance:

> The bears all showed resentment at what they were asked to do. Before coming into the ring they cried out in pain. I slipped to the gangway through which the animals had to pass. I was just in time to see one of the attendants using a short stick with a sharp steel hook at one end. The polar bears are put through their turns by a woman who is much too handy with the whip and stave. The whip lash leaves 'scores' across the coats and occasionally the lash catches them across the face.

The RSPCA inspectors might be considered prejudiced, but Alfred Court, the trainer said:

> The bear had been struck where I had aimed, above the nostrils and between the eyes, blood flowed from its mouth, its paw stiffened and it collapsed.

And a theatre manager has written: 'Three bears were in a cage six feet by three feet where they "lived" all day and all night except for their turn on the stage. Poor creatures, they hated their trainer (Dokhansky) so much that they appeared happy to get back to their minute cages.' In 1965 in the *Daily Mail* Bernard Levin in a feature on the circus entitled 'Farewell without Tears' described bears in bloomers and elaborate 'falsies' riding bikes. The bears retained a noble 'patient dignity' throughout. Levin comments that the appeal to cruelty lies at the root of all circus philosophy, just as people who went to watch and enjoy public floggings enjoyed the humiliation of others.

And so from bears to the big jungle cats, which by their power and ferocity have long been the favourite stock-in-trade of the beast-tamer. Close observation of training methods led us to the surprising conclusion that the animals were far more frightened of their trainer than he was of them. One of the acts we saw 'in rehearsal' was later billed as 'One man alone in a cage full of jungle-bred lions'.

This act appeared to consist of a mêlée of seven or eight young lions who were doing their utmost to get away from the man in the ring cage with them. We later saw the finished act where all the shouting, noise and general air of daring and violence tended to obscure the fact that it was not the trainer who was 'fleeing from his savage charges', but the lions who were doing their utmost to escape from the tamer's attentions. Had we not seen the rehearsing of this act, we might have received the general impression that the man was outnumbered and being very brave. Instead, consider the question voiced by an RSPCA inspector: 'What had gone on in that cage previously to make those lions so anxious to avoid contact with their trainer?'

One of the most famous cat tamers was the celebrated Frenchman, Alfred Court, who has left us frank and detailed comment in his memoirs published in this country under the title *Wild Circus Animals* in 1954. He quotes Dr Goebbels (not a man whom one would expect to be easily shocked) as saying 'I agree it is a sensational act, but what I have against Court is that he is too brutal with his animals'. After this judgment from one of the most ruthless of Hitler's Nazi hierarchy, it is interesting to read Court's own comments:

> The stick and the whip are as necessary as a reward of meat—It was my turn to be brutal, terribly brutal, and brutal I was. All the clubs I had left in the cage were broken one by one on Bengali's head. Lashes came down like an avalanche, cutting deep into the tiger's shining coat …I seized a heavy training stool made of wood and steel, it weighed a good eighty pounds; raising it above my head I flung it at Artis, catching him on the hindquarters. The animal gave a terrible roar, a cry of pain—but the poor beast did not get far, the stool had hit him harder than I intended, snapping his leg.

And so on through a couple of hundred pages. A trainer like Court, matched against fierce jungle beasts, has the crowd on his side. To the gullible onlooker the man may seem a puny creature against the animal he is handling. But the facts are that the odds are almost all on the man's side. He can escape, the beast cannot. He has all the weapons of hunger and attrition to use on the animal. If he tires, someone else can take over until the animal's spirit is broken and he must either give in or die. An ex-circus employee has described to us the methods used to make a leopard 'sit up and beg'. It was chained from either side of its small cage while a man sat just outside and prodded its throat with an instrument like a pitchfork. When the man wearied, another took over. Eventually the leopard would rear up between its two chains at the merest touch of the pitchfork. It had learned its first lesson: man is master and there is no escape. Some few never learn, their spirits are unbreakable, they die of injury or simply of starvation because they are so distraught that they cannot eat. One trainer, describing the long period of spirit-breaking which included withholding food and water stated 'at length they must approach the man or die'. Some—perhaps the lucky ones – just choose to die.

Alfred Court describes how a tiger was billed as 'having already killed three trainers' as a draw to the public. Court reckoned people would pay to see how he proposed to deal with such a man-eater. This gave him *carte blanche* to use any force he liked upon the beast in full view of the public, although he admitted in his book that the statement about the killings was not true.

> I stayed alone with the tigers and punished them in a way they would not forget...Death can only be matched by death and that, when all the trimmings are off, is the lion-tamer's game. He makes the lion perform for profit under the constant threat of death. And the lion is reminded of it by a thousand prods, cuts and lashes. He roars his protest—but he goes through with his act, he does not want to die.

This is not really very far removed from the Roman circus, where beast was set against beast and man against man to give the crowd the thrill of blood.

One reported method of breaking a tiger's spirit before training commences is to spreadeagle it (each paw held tight in a noose) while a good thrashing is administered. At first the animal is furious, a snarling, fighting mass, helplessly trussed. It soon learns that its struggles are hopeless and the beatings continue. Sooner or later the first lesson is assimilated. No matter how brave and fierce you may be, you have no chance against the clever pygmy who has the power of pain and starvation over you.

Many of the complaints of cruelty levelled against circuses are concerned with elephants, whose size and strength would at first sight give an outsider the impression that they are well able to take care of themselves. Their ears and the tender area under the tail are very susceptible to pain and in spite of their great bulk and weight they are amazingly sensitive and intelligent creatures. We learned as much from our visits to winter training quarters. We learned too that the reason why an elephant never evacuates in the ring is that they are 'cleaned out' beforehand.

One of the acts we saw rehearsed was of fully grown elephants standing on one foreleg, an amazing feat of balancing. A veterinary surgeon has pointed out that all the immense weight of stomach and intestines is thus pressing on the animal's heart which, besides being unnatural, is extremely cruel. These ponderous, slow, long-suffering animals are actually 'broken' in Asia before ever they reach these shores. Defendants of circus methods often point out that animals born into close captivity know nothing else and therefore cannot grieve over what they are missing. This does not apply to elephants which have never, to date, been induced to breed in the British Isles. Indeed with one exception (a successful breeding in Switzerland, during the fifties, under perfect control conditions) they have not bred in Europe at all. Capture and breaking and some initial training to make them fit for export is still undertaken in Asia far from any possibility of supervision by any humane society.

The late Colonel Williams, better known as 'Elephant Bill', has described in his books the extremely cruel breaking and training methods employed against elephants and the techniques used to trap and subdue them. Brian O'Brien, an American big game hunter who confesses that his attitude to animals is tough and anything but sentimental was nevertheless so shaken on witnessing some of the methods used in elephant capture and breaking that he wrote a booklet *How to Break an Elephant's Heart*, which does not make pleasant reading. It is now published in England by the Performing Animals Defence League. Another valuable source of evidence is *Elephant Gold* by P. D. Strachey, former Chief Conservator of the Forests of Assam (published in 1963).

And when the raw material arrives from Asia, the ready-broken animal has to learn to perform tricks. To expedite his education, the elephant goad is a useful instrument. A Devon blacksmith, Mr A. Brockhurst from Marldon, near Torquay, explained how he came to supply one of these to a travelling circus that needed to reinforce its equipment:

> I have made some things in my time, so when a length of steel tubing and three inch spike together with a large fish-hook, were delivered to my workshop door, I got on to the job and did as the customer required. After the job was done I enquired what it was all about. I was told that my customer was an elephant trainer and by poking the beast about the ears with the spike end, the animal would roll its head from side to side and swing its trunk like an Indian club. By catching the hook barb under its foot the animal would lift its leg and wave it around. I saw this turn later and, as the trainer bowed his way off after the applause, he waved the goad I had made. There were ribbons flying from its spike and it all looked charming.

Here it is worth noting that elephants, in spite of their huge size and strength, are not in fact immune to pain and suffering. Watching the elephants chained to heavy staples and swinging endlessly from side to side, we began to wonder if we have the right to sentence so many animals to such a life, purely for entertainment. Many other people must have been wondering the same thing, because during the last few years some town councils and local authorities have begun to refuse circuses the use of Corporation land, if performing animals were used. Many school teachers have endorsed this ban, suggesting that the violence and coercion apparent in many acts was not suitable entertainment for children.

The last Act of Parliament that aimed at giving any kind of protection to captive and performing animals was passed on 30 June 1925. Much of its wording sounds like an attempt to protect the trainers and circus proprietors, rather than the animals. Section 3, after declaring that an officer of the local authority and any constable can enter (for purpose of inspection) at all *reasonable times*, goes on to say 'No constable or such officer aforesaid shall be entitled under this section to go on or behind the stage during the public performance of performing animals'. The 'reasonable times' phrase has often been invoked when permission has been sought to inspect some aspect of circus life. It is easy to plead that it is feeding time, or that a very secret act is being rehearsed, and in fact that the time is not reasonable.

On 31 January 1956 Lord Strabolgi 'rose to call attention to the cruelty involved in the training and use of performing animals for exhibition and entertainment purposes; to the general undesirability of such performances; and to their bad effect on children's education'. Lord Strabolgi reminded his listeners of the findings of Sir Peter Chalmers Mitchell (then Secretary of the Zoological Society) to the Select Committee of 1922, which still hold as true today as when he published them:

> You have to get your animals on the stage and do the trick at once, lest the manager and the public be discontented. In my experience there is the greatest possible risk that there has been cruelty, not only in the training, but continuous cruelty in keeping the animal up to the mark for these timed performances. — I do know of some things, which to my mind were so serious, that I told one particular trainer that if he came back to London with this animal, I would have him prosecuted for gross cruelty.

Animals, like human performers, do sometimes have days when they may be unwell or in pain, but they cannot speak. Their trainer is only interested in results, his livelihood depends upon it. But the performing animal must be on top-line performing condition twice nightly and three times on matinee days, and if not he may be punished severely afterwards. It is a moot point here whether the animal does in fact know the reason for the punishment, which may be delivered some time after his act is over.

Lord Strabolgi quoted the case of only a few months before, when at Christmas 1955 2,000 Manchester children at a circus outing saw a tussle between five men and a frightened bear who had failed at his cycling trick. Another incident that same Christmas holiday (the peak time for circuses) was reported by an RSPCA inspector who was present at a public performance.

A lioness, obviously terrified, made frantic attempts to squeeze a way between the bars of the cage, was threatened with the trainer's stick and had to be struck to force it to perform the trick. The sight of a magnificent animal such as this being in terror of a human being is, to put it mildly, pitiful. On the completion of the act, the animals made a mad rush to get through the exit.

Lord Strabolgi commented 'If animals are treated like this in full view of the audience, one shudders to think what they have to undergo when they are out of sight.'

In the 1950s a Senior Inspector of the RSPCA investigated an alleged case of cruelty to a monkey. The trainer explained that it was attacking him and he had to injure it in self-defence. 'It was him or me.' This plea of self-defence is the trainer's main loophole against any law designed to protect captive or performing animals and is successfully invoked on many occasions, which is one reason why so few prosecutions are successfully brought against animal trainers. Another reason is the obvious one that much initial breaking and training, and therefore the worst violence, takes place out of sight of any witnesses other than circus employees.

But Lord Strabolgi's attempt to bring legislation up to date and to offer some real protection to the performing animal met with considerable opposition, not only from the vested interests of the circus industry but from the 'Don't-interfere-with-the-children's-fun' faction.

Supporting the bill was Lord Somers who in 1967 made a telling speech in a personal bid to bring about reform, and introduce fresh legislation. New witnesses were called and up-to-the-minute evidence produced. Among the witnesses was an ex-employee of a large touring international circus, a man called Munslow. He told us that he had left the circus because the cruelty and violence upset him and his wife so much that they decided to quit. He is now driving an ambulance and we talked to him and also made a tape recording which was submitted as evidence. He was not paid, and his comments only came to light because of a letter written to the press about training methods. He wrote to us stating that we had only said what he had known personally for years but that if he tried to tell people what really went on, there was never any reaction of interest. As a beast man he had seen a great deal. His evidence was too long to quote in full. But he referred to a chimpanzee left on a dockside in a crate without food and water for a weekend because none of the dockers would approach it. Munslow himself was sent to collect this animal which he found in a very poor state and almost unable to move. He also cited the case of a baboon which had its fangs removed, so that it could not inflict bites on its trainer, by the simple expedient of being immobilized in chains while the teeth were removed with pliers without anaesthetic. The beast went about holding its face in pain for some days after this and had difficulty in eating. He also described a rosinback which slipped in the ring, colliding with one of the kingposts and badly bruising its face and damaging an eye, but which was made to go on for the second house that night. This bears out the fact that animals are forced to perform even when unwell. He also mentioned the pony that found it difficult to learn and was repeatedly thrashed and how he spent many hours bathing the weals and trying to make it more comfortable. We have seen the wicker cages used to protect the head and eyes when a thrashing is being administered, so as to avoid lasting damage that would result in loss of stock.

When he was asked why he had not given this evidence before, Mr Munslow stated quite honestly that he was afraid to write to the newspapers in case of reprisals upon his family. His wife particularly was very afraid of circus personnel. He said that he only put his evidence before us now because the circus concerned was abroad and there was less chance of reprisal, and his conscience told him he must try to do something for the animals concerned.

In spite of evidence like this, and in spite of many eloquent speeches by Lord Somers and other peers, the measure was defeated by forty-five votes to thirty-one. Leading circus proprietors were present in full force.

In Scandinavia public opinion is ahead of the British Isles, for in Sweden as early as 1944 an Act was passed protecting the rights of captive and performing animals with most stringent regulations and inspection. In 1963 Denmark went a step further, passing an act forbidding the training of animals for exhibitions, circus or film productions, and prohibiting travelling menageries.

It has been said of many kinds of animal exploitation and cruelty that the best way to stop it is not by legislation but by removing the element of profit. The only way this can be done is by the general public staying away from circuses which present animal acts. Some of us do not care to see human performers risk their lives to provide us with thrills, but they are at least compensated according to their skill and daring. The animal is only rewarded with captivity and violence. The human makes a choice, the animal has none.

In 1967 a lion-tamer of Roberts Brothers circus, after having been clawed by one of his lions and finishing his act with his face running with blood, was reported in the press as saying that continentals want to see tricks but British audiences want to be able to say that they almost saw a trainer killed. We think this is true. It is a national characteristic that we can enjoy danger vicariously. Watching men master ferocious jungle beasts probably boosts our ego. But it is just possible that if our children were brought up to believe that animals have some rights, and that cruelty is not a fit spectacle for entertainment, they might find themselves on the beast's side, rather than the tamer's.

We saw Roberts Brothers circus act in 1966 and also toured the menagerie afterwards and wrote to the circus headquarters in the Midlands on our findings, hoping that for the sake of their public image, they would modify some of the conditions under which their animals lived and were transported. We received no reply.

There are trainers who find it possible to establish some kind of rapport with their charges, but they are few and far between. The very nature of the tented circus life of one night stands, or at the most a few days, means little time or patience or energy left over for anything but essentials. Circus life is tough and harsh, and short cuts have to be taken to obtain (and, more important, maintain) the required results. Drugs and electric goads have supplemented the whip and blank cartridge. But observation will still reveal that the big cats have to be prodded and urged into their act in the ring with their master, while their haste to make an exit afterwards says much about how little they enjoy their share of the proceedings.

The presence of an RSPCA inspector may lull the audience into thinking all must be well and no cruelty can be involved or the inspector would interfere. There may be nothing that he can do, for no offence, as the law stands, is being committed. The whips and the goads are only used as reminders of what went before and what will come again if the animal is not instantly obedient. It is a brave man who will go behind the scenes and risk the rough-housing which the roustabouts are only too ready to offer those who interfere.

31

In spite of all this lulling of public opinion, it would seem that circuses are not quite so popular as they once were. Bertram Mills has at long last quit Olympia, the Chipperfield family have taken their animal acts to South Africa, where even there they encountered a good deal of complaint and criticism over their housing of animals in blazing heat on the foreshore at Cape Town. They have a strong footing still in this country, however, with their zoos and animal breeding centres at Plymouth (unsuccessfully opposed by many local people) and Southampton and their partnership with Lord Bath at Longleat.

Several smaller touring circuses remain, including Roberts Brothers, Kays, and the 'Wildest Show on Earth', a mixture of wild west and rodeo. But the real kingpin of British circus now is Billy Smart, who came to the ring comparatively recently when compared with an old 'animal' family like Chipperfields. Smart is nothing if not a showman, and frequent television appearances have kept his name before the public. Few animal performances are included, and those few usually well chosen to give the minimum of offence. In spite of this, the camera does sometimes pick up actions, attitudes or gestures which show that all is not well and that methods have changed very little since that last inadequate Act of 1925. Reinforcing this view is the eye-witness account by Miss Irene Heaton, secretary of the Captive Animals Protection Society, on the Smart Circus at Clapham Common in 1965. She reports on the menagerie thus:

(a) A Civet cat, two or three times the size of a domestic cat, in a cage two feet across by five feet deep, going round and round ceaselessly without hope of release until death. No 'ring' exercise, just solitary confinement.

(b) Tiny monkeys huddled together at back of cage to keep warm on a cold day—mothers with arms round babies.

(c) Polar bears crowded in vans with barely enough room to stretch. No climbing or water facilities as at Whipsnade (or even the London Zoo). The only variation in their existence, the forced entry into the Ring through a tunnel into which they are driven by prods, forks and sticks. One woman assistant's stout ash stick was frayed at the end by constant jabbing. And in the ring, what? More sticks, whips, and an electric goad, a rod with a steel end more than six inches in length, from which I saw a flash, to force the wretched bears on to their stool, up the ladder and down the slide, then prodded back to their prison for the next performance.

(d) Horses fitted with tight bearing reins left without release.

(e) Elephants chained for hours on bare wet floors, no straw, some squealed in pain when attendant caused them to evacuate.

(f) Exposure of sick highland bull in menagerie. This animal had had an internal haemorrhage and a blood transfusion and while still in this state must endure close proximity to gaping crowds and blaring noise.

Those of us who question this type of entertainment are sometimes accused of depriving children of their traditional fun. Perhaps once the Roman circus was also 'traditional fun', and so were bear- and bull-baiting, when the children themselves led lives which were often short, nasty and brutish.

Today's children are no longer so badly in need of this kind of entertainment which, but for doting grandparents providing end-of-term treats, might have died a natural death. Our hope now lies in educating the children towards re-educating their elders. In this way animal acts will become unprofitable, and so the violence and exploitation will cease.

# 2

# *The Bull-fight*

...the Pope wished to abolish it, but the inhuman populace rose up to defend
it, as if the rest of the world should shun the obnoxious profanation, only
Spain could not.

FRAY DAMIAN DE VEGAS, 1590

The mystique that surrounds bull-fighting is rather like the *peto*, or
padded mattress, surrounding the picador's horse – it conceals what,
if openly revealed, would be seen for the thing it is. For in spite of the
*peto*, the horns of the bull still pierce the belly of the picador's horse,
and slit its genitals, till the blood and entrails spill out onto the sanded
floor of the arena in an obscene mess and are pushed back and stitched
up so that the pitiful nag can be returned again to its martyrdom –
but the *peto* hides this, and hides the resulting scars. It seems that
people do not so much mind what goes on if they cannot actually see
it, like the tourist we once had to accompany to a bull-fight in Cordoba,
who, after the picador had inflicted his deep and bloody gash in the
bull's side, said 'Tell me when the wound is not facing us, and I'll
open my eyes.'

Part of the mystique stems from the fact that the Spaniard considers
the bull-fight as an art form, a living art form, *el arte del toreo*, that, so
says the rhyme, was bequeathed from heaven.

The postures, skill, and grace of the torero, like those of some
macabre ballet, are beautiful; there is beauty and excitement in the
charging mass of sheer force, as the bull comes snorting into the arena;
and the very words which describe aspects of the art are beautiful.
The *traje de luz*, 'suit of light' or 'shining raiment' of the torero; the
'moment of truth' – in reality the moment of the kill – which seems to
have something noble and exalted in it; the very name of the passes,
the veronica, for instance, supposed to imitate the position in which
Veronica held the cloth when she wiped the face of Christ on His way
to Calvary; the trainloads of devotees, the *aficionados*, who travel

34

enthusiastically from *corrida* to *corrida*; those ardent, bronzed men in their Cordoban hats who sit hour after hour in the cafés of the Calle de las Sierpes, the Street of the Serpents, in Seville, discussing with fervour and expertise *el arte del toreo*; La Macarena, the Virgin of Hope, the weeping Madonna of the bull-fighters, in the gypsy suburb of Triana; the poems of Garcia Lorca, with their gypsy imagery; and the link in the popular mind between the fire and eroticism of the flamenco dance and the *cante jondo* and the spectacle in the sanded arena – all these are a part of the mystique, the magic, the poetry.

So, is it too, in Central and Southern America. According to 'El Toreo in Mexico' published by the magazine *Artes de Mexico*:

> The Mexican looks at a bull-fight just as at a painting, a church, or a statue. For him the *corrida* is not only a spectacle, a profession or a science, but an art which is accompanied as no other of the arts by tragedy; the constant tragedy of death.

Even the designation of the seats at the bull-ring, *Sol y Sombra*, Sun and Shadow, is pure poetry. Then there is the myth and grandeur of its origins. The first full tournament reported in Spain was about 1100. But from the coronation of Alfonso VII (1701–1719) to the reign of Philip V no public rejoicing was celebrated without the gaudy, exciting spectacle of a bull-fight. Almost certainly, Spain's historic connection with the bull-fight is something far more ancient, stemming from the Minoan rites of Crete, and spreading through North Africa to Spain via the Moorish invasions, or even from the Greek settlers who reached the shores of the Mediterranean littoral. Julius Caesar himself appears to have witnessed some type of bull-fight in Seville, a *taurilia*.

But the bull-fight is big business, on a large scale. Immense fortunes are made out of it, by the millionaire toreros such as El Cordobés, or Juan Belmonte, by the breeders of the 'brave bulls' (*Bos taurus ibericus* being the indigenous bull) on their vast ranches in Andalusia and Estremadura (which, as Thomas Cook's handbook of 1924 points out, 'is the proper occupation of a gentleman', and is so even today), and by the promoters and managers and lawyers. Money is also the concern of the numerous middlemen, and of the journalists, the publishers and advertisers, the humbler souvenir manufacturers and sellers of tourist trinkets – fans, cards, castanets, wallets, bags and purses, decorated with the motifs of the fight (only the more picturesque and pleasing motifs, usually the elegant turns and postures of some gaudy torero) – the travel courier and even the hotel porter who collects his modest commission on obtaining bull-fight tickets for his hotel guests.

In an article 'La Fiesta de los Toros' Gregorio Pablo de Mora writes:

> We have to bear in mind that there are many families—all of them worthy of high esteem—who live out of the fiesta in question; consequently it is not surprising that they should defend it with faith and enthusiasm; yet it may be that there are also those among them who, when they defend it, are defending their livelihood rather than the fiesta

Like all affairs in which huge sums of money change hands, the bull-fight is steeped in corruption—struggling toreros may have to bribe promoters to 'fix' bulls by shaving hooves and cutting horns, administering castor-oil or narcotics, clamping them or raining blows with sand-bags over the kidneys, things that, as John Marks puts it 'were spoken of in whispers, as occurring at dead of night, off-stage.' But now and then these things leak out through the press.

A September 1959 issue of the *New York Times Magazine* published an article entitled 'Enter the Leaden Age of Bullfighting'. It contained some startling revelations. Apparently Manolete, the legendary national hero of the arena, had the horns of the bulls he was to meet shortened by four or five inches just before the combat, so that the bull would be out of range in his lunges.

The Madrid correspondent of *The Times* reported on 1 August 1968 that a fine of six hundred pounds had been imposed by Police Headquarters at Barcelona on Don Pedro Domecq, a well-known breeder of fighting bulls for the arena. He was accused of having supplied for a *corrida* bulls whose horns had been 'artificially modified'. This means blunting the horns by shaving the tips.

The set of six bulls normally used at a *corrida* is worth about a quarter of a million pesetas, or about three hundred pounds for each bull. Between six and seven thousand bulls are now usually killed in Spanish bull-rings each year. In 1930, the last year of the monarchy, 302 full-scale *corridas* were recorded, to say nothing of the innumerable *novilladas* and small village *capeas*. It was twenty years before this figure was again reached, as between the years 1931 and 1935, during the time of the Republic and up to the outbreak of the Spanish Civil War, a drop to some 235 was recorded. However, by the early 1950s this figure had rocketed again to 432 annually—and this when Spain was still a country relatively isolated from Europe, rife with shortages, black-market activities, smarting from the scars and bitterness of the aftermath of its own war and years of political nonrecognition.

Now that some 16,000,000 tourists flock to Spain every year, bull-fighting is bigger business than ever. The same could be claimed for Mexico, where every year more Americans are spending their holidays. Tour companies do not always encourage their clients to patronize the bull-fight, though of course there are some who include bull-fight tickets in their packaged tours.

*The Handbook for Spain of Thomas Cook* (father of all Tour Companies) by Albert F. Calvert, published in 1924 states, when describing the Plaza de Toros in Madrid:

> One is reminded of a scene in the Amphitheatre in the days of the grandeur of Rome, when gladiatorial contests attracted a vast concourse of all classes of the population, for the same love of daring and agility still sways the passion of the people, and the same indifference is evinced when blood flows, provided it be the blood of horses and bulls and not men...

Calvert goes on to write of the bull:

> He has led a placid life on the plains, and has followed the herd-boy as sheep follow a shepherd. But today he must fight and die and, if he is indifferent at the sight of his assailants, means must be employed to anger him.

After describing the terrific vehemence with which the bull charges the picadors, he continues:

> The hapless horses are the worst sufferers, for they cannot escape from the ring. They serve as butts for the bull's horns, being frequently ripped open and sometimes lifted off their feet by the horns of their maddened enemy. To English eyes it is a heart-rending spectacle to see a sorry old horse, which has patiently served man all his life, urged up to the sharp horns of the bull and made to receive his cruel charges. The wounded horses lie quivering and expiring in the ring; a look of supplication and suffering in their eyes fills the unaccustomed spectator with compassion, and the sight of their terrible injuries sickens the sensitive.

It is said on good authority that Queen Ina of Spain wore specially blackened sunglasses when having, from protocol, to attend official *corridas*.

At the great *Feria de Mayo*, the May Fair in Seville, Cook's *Handbook* states:

> To say that the most sanguinary bull-fights complete the festivities is, perhaps, superfluous. The most skilful and renowned toreros are engaged on this occasion and the arenas literally smoke with blood of bulls and disembowelled horses.

In one of the great classics of Spanish literature, *Blood and Sand*, Vicente Blasco Ibañez describes the scene behind the arena:

In the courtyard a group of *aficionados* were watching the picadors trying out their horses. Potaje [the picador] was preparing to mount with a *garrocha* in his hand and great cowboy spurs on his boots. The stable-lads were talking to the contractor who had supplied the horses...

The *monosabios*, with their sleeves rolled up, led out the miserable crocks for the riders to try. They had been training them for several days, and their spur marks still showed red on the wretched animals' flanks. They had forced them to trot with fictitious energy in the open space round the bull-ring, and taught them to turn quickly, so as to get used to their work in the arena. They came back to the stables with their sides covered in blood and were washed down with buckets of water to refresh them. The water running between the cobble-stones and round the drinking trough was dark red, like spilt wine.

Those to be used in the next day's *corrida* were dragged out of the stables, to be examined and passed by the picadors.

These scraggy relics of equine wretchedness came forward with their trembling legs and tortured flanks, presenting a living picture of the tragedy of old age and decrepitude, and of human ingratitude and forgetfulness of past service. Some of them were incredibly thin, mere skeletons whose prominent ribs looked as if they must break through the shaggy hides tightly stretched across them. Others, with shining coats and bright eyes, held themselves proudly, pawing the ground with strong legs; they were splendid animals such as might have come straight from drawing a smart carriage, and seemed quite out of place among their miserable companions. However they were the most dangerous to ride, being afflicted with some incurable disease like the staggers, which meant that they might come down at any moment, sending their riders flying over their heads. Behind these wretched or diseased animals clattered sadly a group of casualties from industry; cab-horses and horses from mills, factories and farms, all worn out from long years spent dragging carts and ploughs: unfortunate outcasts who were to be exploited to the very last moment of their lives, so as to *entertain* human beings by their leaps and kicks of agony when they felt the bulls' horns pierce their bellies!

Here, it is salutary to note that in a television programme, as recently as November 1968, Henry Higgins, the British bull-fighter, commented on the crowd, composed largely of tourists, *laughing* at the antics of a horse lifted off its back legs by the charge of the bull and 'pedalling' in the air. Viewers had seen this incident for themselves when at the beginning of the film the picador was unseated and his horse repeatedly charged and crushed against the barrier, the *peto* hiding all visible signs of damage. Higgins commented that the horse was 'in trouble' but many of the spectators had obviously not realized it and thought that its antics were 'amusing'. So it would seem that little progress, has been made since Ibañez, who goes on to say:

38

It was a procession of galled necks on which bloated green flies were battening; dim eyes with yellowish whites but trustful expressions; long bony heads whose skin was swarming with vermin; angular flanks with coats matted like wool; narrow chests shaken by deep whinnies; feeble legs looking as if they must break at any moment...

John Marks, an expert and devotee of the fight, in his book *To the Bullfight Again* has this to say about the *peto*:

> ...alas, the padded shield, or *peto*, with which the weak-kneed hacks are harnessed for their protection, has nothing whatever to recommend it, except that it was devised with the purest though most misguided of 'humane' intentions.
>
> Today visitors and natives alike seem happily unaware that the protective mattress-covering only serves to guard the managements' business interests and the spectators' sensibilities, by prolonging the miserable existence of a drugged, frightened, beaten, jolted, blindfold, underfed creature, and by sparing the onlooker the ugly sight of major accidents, which constitute the horse's only hope of a speedy and merciful escape from a silent ordeal of nervous anguish, physical pain and internal injury.
>
> The *peto*...is the subtlest instrument of torture that was ever invented by kind-hearted persons...it protracts the moribund horses' lives for an intolerable span of weeks and months, on the hypocritical assumption, that, for all concerned, the animal's slow patient agony is preferable to its violent death in full view of the public.

It was Primo de Rivera, no fan of the fight, who ordained in the twenties that the horses used in the bull-ring must be padded. An RSPCA pamphlet concerned with this decree states:

> The cruelties to horses were too terrible to describe...Hemingway, however, maintained that although the protection prevented the scenes of unmitigated horror and greatly decreased the number of horses killed in the ring, they in no way decrease the pain suffered by horses.

Hemingway, in his *Death in the Afternoon*, describes in some detail these injuries, and the way the horse is stuffed with straw and, roughly sewn, is sent back into the ring again, until it can no longer even stand.

The late Count de Bailén, founder of the Associación Contra La Crueldad En Los Espectatulos, ACCE, wrote in a publication of the Catholic Study Circle for Animal Welfare:

> The public do not realise what horses have to suffer from the moment they arrive at the Plaza de Toros (bull-ring). They ignore what goes on behind the scenes during a *corrida*...The public give no thought to the fact that horses that have been used in one *corrida*, wounded or not, are carted away on lorries to some other bull-ring, and who sees or cares

about how they are treated in transit? Who can read in the tremor of the limbs, in the gnashing of teeth, in the frightened lifting of its head all the terror and pain a horse suffers in the bull-ring?

And what about the central victim of this drama, the bull itself, and the technicalities of the *corrida*?

In an article published in Logroño in 1962, Santiago Esteras Gil asks:

> What has this animal done to deserve such treatment? It was born and bred on the ranch, enjoying the luscious grass of the pasture...He becomes a prisoner in a narrow box. Then comes the jolting of a long journey in a dark box, the incessant shaking of the floor beneath his hooves. The journey ends at the bull-ring.

A law was passed in 1929 in Spain making it illegal for children to attend bull-fights. Under the present regime in Spain this law is no longer in force, and we have seen parties of schoolchildren with teachers watching fights. Children in the United States, perhaps particularly in California, are often able to witness this spectacle, as KHO TV Los Angeles on Channel 9 has hour-long colour bull-fight programmes scheduled at peak viewing times.

Music plays in the Plaza de Toros, the stirring music of the *paso doble* or the quick Spanish march. As Cook's guide has it:

> The tournament opens with an imposing procession of the bull-fighters arrayed in all the glory of the gala costumes, in which there is a plentiful glitter of tinsel and spangles and gold braid.

Two *alguacilas* ride in front of the procession, and the rear is brought up by the *peones* and the gaily decorated mules that are used to drag the corpses of the bulls from the ring. A bugle rings out and the key of the bull's den, or *toril*, is thrown into the arena by El Presidente. Now the first act, or first *tercio*, of the fight takes place, with the torero and his *cuadrilla* playing the bull, and inciting him with their capes. Then comes the second *tercio*, with the picador, whose five-foot lance has a guard on it to limit the depth of penetration. The rules actually dictate that the picador should inflict the wound in the withers, but as the renowned French *aficionado*, Ernest Fornairon, who boasts of having viewed the killing of more than a thousand bulls since 1912, writes:

> The picador's act has become in our days pitiful murder...the picadors do their best to cripple the bull by wounding him in the backbone or in the shoulder, or they twist the shaft with the object of making a deep wound and endeavour to plant the weapon several times in the same place.

As well as sustaining the repeated pressures and charges of the bull against the lance, the exhausted, skeleton horse must bear not only the weight of the picador himself – which is usually very substantial – but also the eighty pounds of protective 'armour' which the picador wears, and a heavy cowboy-type saddle which causes the animal great bruising whenever it crashes down in the arena. One famous gypsy picador witnessed the killing of 120,000 horses in the process of killing only 30,000 bulls.

In the third *tercio* it is the job of the *banderilleros* – sometimes of the torero himself – to impale the charging bull on cheerily decorated sticks, usually three pairs, which are two to three feet long, with barbed points five inches in length.

Then follows the fourth *tercio* with the romantic 'Moment of Truth', the culmination of the drama, when the victorious torero will attempt to kill the bull with his sword.

In the words of John Marks: 'The matador's job is done when the bull, wounded by his sword, sinks to its knees.' Often the attempts are bungled or do not strike home, and many thrusts have to be made before it collapses.

A report published in 1962 by a member of the Royal College of Veterinary Surgeons, has this to say:

> Sighting along the spine, the matador plunges a thirty-inch-long sword between the bull's shoulder blades, aiming to puncture the heart. Sometimes the bull falls dead on the spot after a single stroke; more often several thrusts are needed to despatch the doomed animal. If the sword fails to pierce the heart or sever the aorta, the bull may slump helplessly to the ground, and vomit with blood pouring from its nostrils. The matador will then withdraw the sword and plunge it in again, as often as necessary – until the great blood vessels have been cut and the bull lies dead at his feet. In one case that I witnessed, eight thrusts were needed to kill.

Sometimes the lungs are pierced, and blood flows frothily from the mouth. In his book, *L'Envers de la Corrida*, Fornairon wrote:

> In the last minute before the kill, the animal is quite exhausted, not only physically; it has also lost the use of its senses, its sight has almost gone…These modern show bull-fighters avail themselves of its somnolent state to execute their 'flourishes' in safety.

If the torero cannot manage to get the bull killed in the prescribed time, it has to be finished off by the butcher's knife. Afterwards the bull is dragged out by the galloping mule team with their yellow and red bobbles flying, and is cut up to be sold as cheap meat from the bull-ring *matadero*. As Dennis Potter write in *The Times Saturday Review* of 16 November 1968 'Nobody shouts an "Olé" when the executed bull is dismembered into steaks and warm offal.'

Robert Graves once claimed that 'If it were not for tourists, the rings would stay almost empty.' This may be a debatable point, but it is probably not debatable to say that the vast influx of tourists has to some extent debased the standard of the bull-fight. When the performance is not before a selected audience with judgment, knowledge and discrimination of some of the finer points of *el arte de toreo*, there is an increase in the frequency of suffering endured by the bulls through bungled killings and wrong and undue wounding, as well as added injury and torture for the horses— all under cover of the *peto*, of course.

Ibañez, in *Blood and Sand*, described these last moments like this:

> Some of the swords hardly penetrated the flesh and fell out almost immediately, others stuck quivering in a bone with most of their length exposed. The bull made the rounds of the barrier, bellowing with his head low, as if complaining of this useless torment. The matador followed, muleta in hand, longing to put an end to it, and yet terrified of exposing himself to danger, and behind him came a troup of peones flourishing their capes as if trying to persuade the animal to double its legs and collapse on the sand. As the bull went by with foam falling from its muzzle and its neck bristling with swords, there was a further explosion of jeers and insults. 'It's like La Dolorosa!'* someone cried. Others compared it to a pincushion full of pins.

It is an as yet unexplained, perhaps unexplored, phenomenon, that in this age which prides itself on its humanitarianism, bull-fighting is a cult, a craze. Tauromachy clubs are springing up everywhere, and there are attempts to introduce it to such unlikely settings as Mozambique and Moscow. Efforts have been made to start it in Japan, and the Argentine Association for the Protection of Animals, among others, made strong representations to the Japanese SPCA in Tokio. The Spanish season (as opposed to the French regional style where the bull is never injured,) in the south of France opens enthusiastically in Arles at Easter, then at Ceret, Frezensac, Béziers, Bordeaux, Bayonne, Dax and Nîmes, and continues until October. Irwin Shaw, the American novelist, went to Nîmes to see the three days of the Feria in which El Cordobés was taking part. He paid $100 for mediocre seats for the three days, and the Roman arena at Nîmes, which holds 25,000, was filled to overflowing each day. A little multiplication will show the

_____
* Virgin of Seven Sorrows, with swords piercing her heart.

immense sums of money changing hands for seats alone, to say nothing of the behind-the-scenes financial manipulation.

This is true also in the Latin American countries, Peru, Venezuela and Ecuador, and particularly Mexico, where the Sunday afternoon bull-fights are included in packaged tours, and are packed with North American tourists. Mexico has some eighty bull-rings, a season extending in Mexico City from October to March, and elsewhere throughout the year, and over a hundred ranches where the brave bulls are bred. In an article in ISPA, Luisa Guijarro Haas, whose father founded Mexico's first Humane Society in 1941, says that because their popularity is growing at a rapid pace, fostered by an increasing number of television stations telecasting bullfights, and the tremendous number of Californians frequenting bull-fight arenas in neighbouring Mexican towns, 'it is not unlikely that in the foreseeable future bull-fights will be legalized in California.' So far Argentina and Uruguay have defeated and resisted hard pressures on their Humane Laws which forbid bull-fighting. The Mexican interest in the fight, or the kind of tolerance which allows a very trendy restaurant in Mexico City featuring 'do-it-yourself' bull-fighting to flourish on US tourists, was satirized by Tom Lehrer in a song in which he refers to running down a dog with his car and being 'awarded the ears and tail' (traditional reward of the matador) for consummate artistry, so putting the cult in its true perspective as wanton killing.

Possibly Hemingway started the cult in the Paris of the twenties, and he has been followed by a string of famous people. Padre Laburo, a fervent *aficionado*, an editor of the Spanish magazine *Digame*, said that bull-fighting 'might become international, that is to say, might reach all corners of the earth'. All the indications are that the trend is spreading, and that Great Britain is by no means immune.

In 1947 the BBC broadcast a running commentary by Edward Ward from a bull-fight and in recent times has put out detailed television films. A coloured film was also shown on various cinema circuits, and a bull-fight was one of the attractions of the very first Cinerama production.

Vincent Hitchcock, the first British matador, was lauded in the British Press, and the incident of Miguelin kissing the bull which El Cordobes was fighting — 'in view of many British tourists' — was widely reported. Henry Higgins, perhaps a more sympathetic character than Vincent Hitchcock, stated after his British television appearance that to him bull-fighting was the kind of challenge other Englishmen usually find in climbing Everest or challenging the sea.

Children in Spain may be seen charging each other with wickerwork replicas of bulls' heads over their faces, or an improvised pair of horns, to practise making passes—often done with the amazing skill of imitative youth.

During the impromptu *corridas* that are a feature of many small-town fiestas, anybody who wants to can jump into the arena to challenge the bull, usually very young, a yearling provided by some local rancher or by the municipal authorities, in the same way that they would provide fireworks or bands. At these impromptu *corridas*, bull-fighters of promise are sometimes spotted.

The same type of 'free-for-all', on a much rowdier, more tumultuous, dangerous and sanguinary scale takes place at Pamplona—and has since the days of Charlemagne—to celebrate the fiesta of San Fermin, and, with variations, at a few other provincial towns. About a dozen bulls are let loose in the streets and chased and harried and wounded with cudgels, darts and spears: an uninhibited and savage piece of blood-letting that goes on until far into the night. In recent years some of these fiestas have been modernized and the spearing is allowed to be done from jeeps and tractors.

However, a young American friend of the authors did not train in any of these rough-and-ready ways; he attended a school of Tauro-machy, where he learnt to make passes and to stick darts and swords into a cork and wicker bull effigy which was trundled about the school arena by a sweating youngster. Also, as the foreign organization for which he worked was well-known and popular in Spain, some cattle breeders allowed him to practise 'live' on their ranches, with the *garrocha* or bull-lance, or in the small private corrals which they often construct on their own land.

We felt about as nervous as our friend Vince himself must have done, watching his début in the provincial ring which was holding a series of *novilladas* for the local patron saint. At these *novilladas* the bulls are small and young, the picadors mostly dispensed with, and the *traje de luz*—a very expensive outfit costing upwards of £120—is not worn, the bull-fighters preferring the leather trousers and short suede bolero jacket of the herdsman. Altogether there is less pomp and ceremony and much more rough horse-play, which often takes the form of a *Charlotada*, or type of bull pantomine, in which clowns rush into the ring dragging the bull by the tail and pushing it by the horns, buffeting it with gaudy sandbags, balloons and strings of sausages, letting off firecrackers under its hooves and tying fireworks onto its horns, so that even the creature's usually bungled death is robbed of any dignity,

44

and its blood and fear are turned to a comic burlesque, of infinite pathos.

I might add that Vince did not show any prowess in the ring, and was trampled on and tossed by the small, frisky animal. His wounds were, however, surprisingly slight, and what suffered most was his elegant leather costume, ripped to pieces. It is always said that wounds from the bulls' horns heal remarkably rapidly, and it was certainly true in his case. Penicillin is so much a part of the bull-fight now that Alexander Fleming might be called the patron saint of toreros, and in fact there is a statue to him in Madrid outside the bull-ring.

In contrast to the rather squalid *novilladas* there is the dashing style of fighting, derived from the Portuguese (where the bull is killed in view of the public at the end), called *Rejonear*, featuring daring feats of skilled 'Highschool' horsemanship on wonderful, fast horses trained to the last inch. Three five-foot lances are broken into the back of the bull's neck, each time leaving a seven-inch, two-edged blade in the wound, and three or four pairs of banderillos with hooks on the end are plunged in, often at full gallop, and while letting the reins go. Peralta, one of the greatest *rejoneadores*, sometimes stuck a red rosette onto one of the bull's wounds, at full gallop of course, to the standing ovation of the crowd.

In *The Spanish Riding School*, Princess Mathilde Windisch-Graetz describes how the Lipizzaners toured Andalusia with their displays of Haute Ecole:

> But as no Feria would be complete without the excitement of a series of bullfights, the same crowd returned next day to give vent to their emotion and enjoy an *additional treat*. After the fourth bull had played his first and last act to the cheers of a packed amphitheatre, the sound of trumpets heralded the entry of a rider and his great mare Liron for a one man show—the doors of the bullpen opened once again to release *another baffled victim*. For a moment or two the 'Rejoneador a caballo' and the *small black bull* stood facing one another. In the fight that followed Don Angel Peralta not only used 'bandelliras' (darts) for baiting the bull and 'rejoneillos de castigo' (harpoons) *for dazing him* but performed practically all the movements of the haute ecole to avoid him by a hair's breadth each time he charged. Angel Peralta manœuvered his mount so brilliantly as to meet the final attack of the bull on the horses's flank when, with no seconds to spare, he drove his short spear into the one fatal spot to deliver the deadly blow.

Other famous *rejoneadores* were Juan Belmonte, Count Alvaro Domecq of the sherry family, the Duke of Piñohermoso, and the beloved, beautiful blonde, Conchita Cintrón. Señora Cintrón was born in Peru and from being a superb horsewoman she graduated to fighting bulls in the old way, on horseback. Fortuna saw her and insisted that she face bulls on foot to prove herself. She has declared that 'We die for some-thing – the bull has no intelligence and lives only to die'. But in her memoirs, *Torera*, she is anthropomorphic enough to elevate the bull to a tragic hero and to make him an equal protagonist in the lethal encounter. It is as if she imagines a dialogue accompanying this bloody ritual between them. But Dennis Potter, in his review of the book referred to earlier, comments 'The bull totters, spews blood and sprawls on the scuffed sand. It does not say anything, and speech is the first requisite of a tragic hero'. There is no man in the beast and we are left only, as Ibañez has noted, with the beast in man.

Beauty, daring and pageantry are powerful analgesics that also act on the Spanish Government itself:

> It [the bull-fight] combines certain essential elements of courage, danger, skill and grace, which together constitute an art. If any of these elements are lacking, the Bull-fight becomes nothing more than the cruel slaughter of a brave animal. From *Home Office Order*, official gazette of the Spanish State, 11 February, 1953.

# 3

## Rodeos and Show Jumping

'The Colt that backed and burdened being young
Loseth his pride and never waxeth strong.'
                    SHAKESPEARE, VENUS AND ADONIS

In Britain, immediately after the war, agricultural shows flourished as
never before. They were the shop window for a newly-affluent farming
industry where every manufacturer of machinery, fertilizer or seed-
dressing wanted a stand. To the farming community it was the family
day out, and townsmen, clamped to their city by long years of austerity,
also found them a breath of fresh air.

During the fifties attendances began to fall, and this, together with
the ever-rising costs of presenting such shows, caused the organizers
to look round for new attractions to raise extra revenue. There was
always a nucleus of faithful supporters and exhibitors, but to draw a
wider crowd some extra inducement was needed, something new,
something different.

In Britain the Cinematograph Films (Animals) Act of 1937 rendered
'broncho busting' illegal, although at least one travelling exhibition of
this kind, known as 'Broncho Bill's Circus' got away with it well into
the sixties. The cinematic ban does not extend to the import of feature
films such as *Ben Hur*, *Genghis Khan*, *The Charge of the Light Brigade*
and *War and Peace*, filmed on location (Spain being a favourite country
for this type of epic) where there are virtually no animal protection
laws and where crashing falls and tightly reined-in, foaming-at-the-
mouth steeds are part of the thrill and spectacle as they are to a lesser
extent in many westerns. Our closer association with the cult of the
western via the medium of television will reveal that the horse is often
an integral part of the action and in a most gruelling rôle. Even allowing
for speeded-up sequences and faked stunts, a straight look at the horse
rather than its star rider (or his stand-in) will show riding methods and

severe bitting and reining-in at speed worthy of Genghis Khan or some Arab sheikh. We would compare some of the curb bits to be seen in, for instance *The Virginian* (an extremely well-made western series) with some of the harsh types used in the Middle East, capable of exerting extreme leverage against tongue and lower jaw and giving the impression that the horse's mouth is being sawn in two.

It was in this context that rodeos, or the British version of wild west shows, were introduced. There was opposition from the start, often from people who had some experience of this kind of spectacle in America and Canada.

The West Country, with its access to rough, unbroken ponies, be-came the first stronghold of this new show attraction. Most spectators probably thought that the young men 'having a go' on these wild steeds were being heroic, and, after being nurtured on a diet of television westerns, saw nothing wrong in this particular exploitation of horseflesh. The participants, too, probably saw the rodeo only as a challenge to their daring and courage and as a possibility of winning acclaim and perhaps a money prize.

In 1965 the National Council for the Study of Animal Welfare reported a campaign by a Cleveland attorney and some members of the Ohio House of Representatives to clean up rodeos by preventing 'the use of twisted wire snaffles, bucking straps, electric prods or similar devices, all of which are standard equipment for making animals perform in rodeos'.

A horse will kick up its heels and lash out to try and unseat an un-welcome rider, but to ensure continuous bucking of a very high order, making it almost impossible to stay on for the requisite length of time (such performances are timed), extra irritants must be applied. The most usual is the cinch, or bucking strap, fastened tightly into the groin and over the back of the saddle causing the animal to plunge and buck madly in an effort to free itself of the painful pressure. Other inducements to buck are caustics applied to genitals or rectum which cause the horses to contort themselves in an effort to find relief. All this looks wildly funny to the ignorant spectator. Electric prods or goads can be used to ensure that calves and steers, during calf-roping or steer-wrestling demonstrations, dash out from the pen gates full-force into the arena to inject proper life into the proceedings.

The Calgary stampede is probably the best known of this type of show. In rich wheat, cattle and mining country, Calgary goes berserk in a boomtown, carnival atmosphere with prize money of over £20,000 at stake. Sensation-seekers are amply catered for with fast chuck-wagon

*Above*
Performing horses in a circus. Training methods are often cruel and barbaric.
*(Photopress)*

*Below*
The mass death of pigs on a factory farm. (*Wiltshire Constabulary*)

*Above*  An incident at Becher's Brook in the Grand National. (*Sunday Mirror*)

*Below*  The end of a day's sport. A fox is thrown to the hounds.
(*Syndication International*)

racing and a 'wild horse race'. It is a prior condition of this last event that the horses must not have been 'touched by human hands' before being conveyed to the stampede. It does not require much effort of imagination to picture the terror and panic during transit and in the course of the event. The race is a team feature as it takes three men to catch each horse when it comes tearing into the arena. One man grabs the halter and anchors the rope, the second throws on the saddle, and the third mounts and attempts to ride to the finishing line.

American films and television showings of these wild west shows reveal a good many of these abuses for those willing to use their eyes. The cinch is almost always visible if you look carefully; often the leather strap is the same colour as the horse, but it is still quite detectable if you look at the animal's hindquarters rather than having your eyes riveted to the man on horseback, hanging on like grim death.

American riders only have to remain on horseback eight seconds to qualify. The English rodeo lets the participant stay on until unseated, and in place of the strong 'broncho' often uses small semi-wild ponies off the moor, ill-nourished and probably suffering from worm infestation. Completely inexperienced riders hang on, not by the reins, but by grasping handfuls of the animal's mane, which in some cases is pulled out in large tufts.

The Shepton Mallet Mid-Somerset Show of August 1965 drew the following item by George Halliday in the *Western Daily Press*:

> Dartmoor ponies should not be used in a rodeo in Shepton Mallet next week. Mrs Barbara Macdonald, Secretary of the Dartmoor Livestock Protection Society, says this in a letter to the Western Daily Press.
>
> 'Will the exploitation of our Dartmoor ponies never stop?' Advertisements, says Mrs Macdonald, proudly proclaim that they come straight off the moor and have never been ridden. Any volunteer will be invited to "have a go".
>
> 'These unbroken ponies have travelled a minimum of seventy miles by road, and they will have been rounded up and loaded; pushed into a collecting yard, and then into the "box" before being dropped on to by the intrepid volunteer', says Mrs Macdonald. 'They will be let loose into the ring, surrounded by a shouting crowd. The Protection of Animals Act 1911, makes it an offence to either infuriate or terrify an animal. And no one who knows anything about unbroken moorland ponies is going to believe that this sort of exhibition will do neither.'

*The Times* of 23 January 1968 showed a photograph of a rodeo in the United States revealing a good deal of dust and violence, one 'broncho' on the ground, a group of men hauling on the reins of another to drag it in. Beside this, the West Country version may appear comparatively tame, but hefty young men clinging to the manes of wild Dartmoor ponies are not an edifying spectacle. In the 1911 Act the term 'over-ride' is used. It may have been aimed originally at owners who rode horses to death for a wager (or until they dropped) on the hunting field – an all-too-frequent occurrence well into this century. But many hold it is no less a case of over-riding when large heavy youths hang on to small un-broken ponies amid the roars of applause from the crowd. One horse coper from the far west keeps a team of these rodeo ponies which he carts round the country at some profit to himself. Whether, strictly speaking, they remained wild and unbroken at the end of a long season (agricultural shows go on from May to September) is open to doubt. Breaking, i.e. getting a horse used to bridle, saddle and eventu-ally a rider, should be conducted with patience, skill and quiet firm-ness', all qualities conspicuously missing from these new exhibitions.

Show jumping, on the other hand, has for many years been an established favourite as a spectator sport. Perhaps it was television with its meticulous recording of these equestrian events that first made the man in the street conscious of their excitement. Their popularity has been one of the surprises of the 'goggle box', and people who scarcely know one end of a horse from another can watch with bated breath the finer points of Wembley or the White City events, while the Horse of the Year Show causes almost as much excitement in the TAM ratings as a television Cup Final.

Competitive jumping has long been a feature of agricultural shows. After the prize-beasts have been judged and the exhibits toured, the grandstand fills up and the entire perimeter of the show ring is densely lined for this absorbing spectacle.

In the 1950s hundreds of country children made Pat Smythe their heroine, while many a point-to-pointer must have hoped to find another Foxhunter to make his name and fortune. A select band of riders and their mounts became household names. Again, as in rodeos and in performing animal acts, the general public saw only what they wanted to see.

One heard of tempers lost behind the ring, but there was more often than not an RSPCA inspector to keep a friendly eye on the proceedings and discourage any ungentlemanly (or unladylike) behaviour. But when money and professionalism enters into any kind of competitive sport, attitudes change. At one large show we saw a young rider being booed by the spectators because he whipped and spurred his horse incessantly the whole way round the course. He was red in the face as much from temper as exertion. Considering the onlookers were fellow countrymen and the rider was known to many of them, it indicates the innate sense of fair play still left in respect of our proper treatment of animals. But, far from improving, this sense has deteriorated in the face of increased pressure from financial gain.

In October 1961 a team of Army horsemen put on a display, including a musical ride at Windsor Horse Show. One of the horses was out in his timing and made a mistake. Afterwards he was schooled by his rider with the aid of a member of the British Show Jumping Association. During the schooling, the horse was thrashed with a stockwhip, brought up by another horseman.

Bystanders and stockmen, tending their beasts which are part of the Show exhibits, gave witness that the horse was most cruelly treated. The phrase 'running it into the ground' was used, and one stockman was reported as saying 'If we used our beasts like that we should be sent to jail'. However, a veterinary surgeon who examined the horse later, found insufficient evidence of cruelty and the three men were acquitted.

We found this view strongly reinforced only a few months later, when in the words of Clifford Luton in the *Daily Express*: 'International show rider Frederick Edgar was suspended last night by the British Show Jumping Association because of "conduct offensive to the public" '. This was the same man who had helped the cavalry man chastise his mount after the alleged mistake.

After these cases we thought that those in charge of such events might be more watchful, and this in fact proved to be so. For at Castle Cary (Somerset) horse show in 1965 a Cornish rider was severely reprimanded by a Show steward for the way he used his mount. The steward was himself a member of the BSJA and not a prejudiced onlooker. The local press noted that the horse had returned with its owner to Cornwall 'for further schooling'. It is not difficult to imagine what those innocuous few words actually entailed for the horse. The case was not followed up, and no doubt the rider and the horse appeared in other shows to other spectators ignorant of the reputation acquired at Castle Cary.

In 1966 the Equestrian Correspondent of *The Times*, who had always delivered extremely interesting accounts of the major show jumping events, weighed in with an article drawing attention to bad practices in the ring. In an effort to exert absolute control, essential in split-second timing, awkward obstacles and tight turns, horses were being half throttled, he wrote. The television viewer, watching these events and hearing the stertorous breathing of the horses, might be forgiven for thinking this was just natural breathlessness at the sustained exertion. Closer observation might reveal that many of these horses were so severely bitted as to be held literally 'in irons'. Following the Equestrian Correspondent's feature, the chairman of the BSJA, Mr James Barrie, replied, refuting the allegations and expressing surprise that they were ever made. It is interesting to note that among the points made in his letter Mr Barrie stated: 'Obviously in a sport with more than five thousand active participants there are bound to be a few who do not conform to the spirit of the sport and from time to time transgress'.

How many is a few? and how often do they transgress? He went on to say:

> It is not possible to answer all the allegations and insinuations contained in the article, but it might be worth mentioning that in recent weeks a complaint about an international rider at Ascot was dismissed after an investigation lasting more than two hours; and a complaint of excessive use of spurs outside the ring was investigated within minutes by both a veterinary surgeon and an independent judge and proved to be unfounded. On the other hand a recent complaint of misuse of spurs was upheld by the stewards and the rider immediately suspended.

A great many people hold the view that a horse which will not jump satisfactorily without the use of spurs should not be jumping at all. Underneath Mr Barrie's letter appeared another, written by a Mr van de Kasteele, of Tavistock, which upheld the findings of *The Times* Correspondent:

> I would like to congratulate your Equestrian Correspondent on the two excellent articles about the mistreatment of Show jumpers (September 30th and October 4th).
>
> For some years I travelled a show jumper myself, and am now a B.S.J.A. judge, and like everyone connected with the sport am fully aware that these practices go on. I have made protests at shows and at B.S.J.A. meetings and always these have been brushed aside.
>
> In common with many friends I am now so sickened that I feel like leaving the stands when the jumping starts, and I cannot understand why the B.S.J.A. is not more concerned with the good name of their sport. Of course the inspection of horses' legs at Wembley is a complete farce when competitors are forewarned. I would like to see spot checks at all major shows with *no* warnings, and a rule long overdue that any horse obviously sore or lame should be disqualified.
>
> I would like to see the same thing applied to horses leaving the ring with blood coming from either their mouths or spur marks, and *regular* inspection of the horse lines during *non show* hours when misuse of stick and cruel schooling practices are all too common.

Much of the cruel schooling referred to takes place in the 'collecting ring' before jumping starts. This is really a warming-up process before the event. Some riders make up for lost time by excessive schooling at the last moment, taking short cuts to the finished product by the use of gadgets. A dropped noseband, known as a grackle, is a mechanical aid to horse control, which is so important in successful jumping but which should be achieved by long and patient schooling.

More knowledgeable members of the public have complained about half-throttled horses with grackles spoiling their pleasure in the show jumping events at our agricultural shows. One answer is to have some ruling and supervision over the type of tack used on show jumpers, even at the smaller agricultural shows, and much more strict stewarding in the collecting rings and around the show ground. A little warming-up is necessary, but a horse that has not been properly schooled at home is not going to reach a very much higher standard suddenly in the last hour or two before it enters the ring.

The inspection of legs referred to in *The Times* letter was a direct outcome of *The Times* articles which stated that 'A mild turpentine blister is a well-known means of teaching a horse not to hit fences'.

These blisters, which can also be caused by other agents, including direct burning with a hot iron, may be hidden under the normal leg bandages. The horse will give just that extra lift to avoid contact with the top bar on a tender spot, thus giving the rider a coveted clear round.

After the article, when the Horse of the Year Show opened at Wembley the President of the BSJA, Col. Mike Ansell, announced that he had decided to instruct the honorary veterinary surgeon to inspect the legs of certain bandaged horses in each jumping competition.

*The Times* correspondent comments:

The general feeling among riders seems to be that this inspection is long overdue. But it may well defeat its own ends in that the less reputable practitioners have been forewarned.

The owner of a badly blistered horse is unlikely to risk apprehension, even though the odds against his being detected are fairly long, with only two horses coming under surveillance at each competition. No doubt it will be announced at the end of the week that not a single horse was discovered with blistered legs. This will not prove that the practice does not exist but simply that officialdom is burying its head in the sand.

It is nevertheless encouraging that steps are at last being taken to do away with this particular aspect of cruelty to show jumping horses, which has caused much distress to horse lovers over the past few years.

In order to make every appearance of concern over its own good name the B.S.J.A. makes "a show of catching a few minnows but lets the real sharks escape. Constant vigilance and immediate action is the only answer".

A long article by Lieut.-Col. C. E. G. Hope, Editor of *The Light Horse*, details many cases of abuse, lost tempers, and punishment which he has himself witnessed. Typical is the case of a rider who, returning from a faulty round, first beat the horse and then kicked it for an appreciable time on the cannon bones. He observes that often stewards and judges do nothing to interfere (it is almost as if they fear to draw attention to such conduct). Col. Hope quite rightly states that 'the real trouble is the misuse and mistreatment of horses in the mistaken idea that it will make them do better in the show ring and no doubt make more money.'

This is the crux of the whole matter. When jumping was a friendly competition and not the matter of life and death which makes it so absorbing to watch, the horse was given a chance to show what he could do within his own capacity. Now he often has to do what is expected or suffer the consequences.

The pressure upon international show jumpers and their mounts, particularly in such status-making events as the Olympic Games, is terrific. With so much at stake, blind eyes can be turned and permissive attitudes adopted.

At the Olympic Prix des Nations show-jumping in the Mexico 1968 Olympics, Marion Coakes' pony Stroller was so sick with an abcess in the mouth that she had nearly had him scratched, the previous week. Speaking of the fences and the course, the toughest in show-jumping, she said: 'It looked a big fence to any horse, but to Stroller it was Mount Everest.' Stroller is 14.2 hands high and the fences rose to five feet four inches, apart from tricky triple jumps, where he hit a fence and was knocked over by falling logs.

Afterwards, as the *Daily Mail* reported, Marion Coakes said: 'Poor Stroller has been quite ill. I almost made up my mind to scratch a week ago and that would have been heartbreaking. He had a bad abcess in the mouth but a veterinary surgeon gave him injections to deaden the pain and to bear the bit. Only great courage kept Stroller going over those difficult fences and on a tight course packed with noisy spectators.'

Who can say again, after this naïve admission, that show-jumping is free from abuse?

Perhaps this question of the undue exploitation of the horse, for

54

money or for personal and national prestige, came through to the general public for the first time at the 1968 Olympics in Mexico, through the media of television and graphic reporting, and many began to ask themselves whether this type of punishing event which exposes horses to too stringent training methods, to danger, injury, excessive overstrain—which can add up quite simply to cruelty—was really justified.

The crowning irony is that the horse is not naturally a jumping animal, especially with a heavy weight upon its back. A senior RSPCA official has explained that it is the cloven-hooved deer, goats and ungulates who are nature's high jumpers. Their type of hoof gives spring in taking off and landing, a natural spring completely denied the horse who often lands with a heavy jarring shock, which explains the strains and sprains to which he is prone.

In the increasingly competitive field of the turf, pursuit of success and large fortunes will lead some trainers and jockeys to resort to anything in order to win, and the horse is usually the sufferer. Even in flat racing, horses are sometimes required to expand themselves too fully too young, while steeple chasing produces bad incidents year after year. It can be said that the riders risk their necks too, but they have a free choice and commensurate reward.

Year after year the press carries photographs of rolling horses, legs thrashing the air, telling their own story of injury and damage in steeple-chasing, point-to-point racing and cross-country events, over stiff jumps and gruelling courses. At Catterick racecourse in 1968 five horses died in one day. According to the *Daily Mail*, Major Leslie Petch, Catterick's managing director, said: 'Jockeys and trainers agreed that it was just sheer bad luck. It was generally agreed that the jockeys took these inexperienced jumpers at the fences much too fast.'

This seemed to raise hardly a murmur of public protest, and yet if the same racegoers had as tourists seen five horses killed in a single afternoon's bull-fighting, they would undoubtedly have thought *that* wrong.

There are momentary outbursts of public indignation, as in 1951 when only three horses finished the gruelling, thirty-jump course of the Grand National at Aintree, and again in 1959 when only four finished and several horses had to be shot for injuries.

Other forms of horse racing do not advertise their cruelties so much to the public. Anyone can witness a steeplechaser breaking a back in full view of the TV cameras. In Britain we largely know of 'walking horses' or trotting races from imported films, and while some have doubts about the methods employed to get a horse to 'pick his feet up' to the extent displayed, they have no personal knowledge of the methods employed. We quote therefore from a report compiled by the Canadian Wild Horse Society of 1968:

> When his front feet are tender, the horse puts his rear feet as far as possible under him to support his weight, this lowers the rump giving the desired walking-horse conformation. And it puts him in such a position that he throws his front feet out further in the ring, this makes a real prancer of him—To make him throw his feet out still further he is frequently trained with chains round his feet. He tries to throw off the chains as he walks, giving him a longer kick with his front feet. If the "ankles" have been *sored* first usually with oil of mustard or some other "burning" agent, the chains will add to the soreness and make the horse move more tenderly—a short cut to the finished result. In the ring chains are forbidden of course but according to this Society they can be replaced with leather boots which slide up and down over the sored parts, having the same effect. One trainer is quoted as saying "These are man-made steps, the front hooves are elongated and weighted so the horse has to throw his foot even to move it. I know one trainer who puts 6 lbs of weight on each hoof." The weights would not appear to be so barbaric as the insistence on *soring*. To this end the "boots" may be aided in their work by being roughly lined, with tacks or barbs or a horseshoe nail may be driven into the quick of the foot causing immediate soreness, burning agents include oxide of mercury known as 'creeping cream.'

The Congressional Record of 10 May 1966 contains particulars of eye-witness accounts by the American Humane Association and the Chattanooga Humane Educational Society of preparations before the 'National Celebration of the Walking Horse, Shelbyville, Tenn. on 4 September 1965':

> The mare was in pain, closed her eyes, breathed hard, tucked her hind feet in front of her, moaned and tried to lie down. They started to cut her feet and I have never seen a horse with its feet cut so deep or the frog cut as this mare. A twitch had been put on her lip and the trainer held the mare's head throughout the torture. The blacksmith took up an electric torch, ground it on to the mare's shoe and burned her foot. They poured water on the foot and it steamed. When the mare was led back to her stable she could not walk but slid down trying to protect her sore feet. Later I saw her ridden in the ring—she gave a beautiful performance, flowing, barely touching the ground with her fore feet.

To display dressage and Haute Ecole training carried to its highest degree of complete mastery over the horse, there is the Spanish Riding School in Vienna, a kind of dilettantes' circus which illustrates some of

56

the most powerful aspects of man's dominion over the horse, while disguising it by the fairytale unreality of the setting and presentation.

Haute Ecole stemmed from the old manuals of horse training perfected to protect the rider in times of war. In the *pescade*, the horse rears up with its head above the level of the rider, an effective shield; the difficult *capriole* brings the rider down on a fallen enemy with lethal force; and many of the other movements were guaranteed to strike terror into the hearts of the infantry or to facilitate, by sudden controlled leaps, the advance or retreat in moments of emergency, to help save the rider's life.

Today the heirs of this long warlike tradition, the white 'Lipizzaners', a pure Spanish-Arab breed, put on displays in Vienna. Many Americans, when booking European tours, specify that they should include tickets to The Spanish Riding School. So these performances are booked up solidly for many months ahead, rather as the Shakespeare Memorial Theatre is at Stratford-upon-Avon, being made a main purpose of the tour. Tourists will go to any lengths to secure admission to this spectacle and will queue for hours just to see the stables.

The wonderful theatrical setting of Fischer Von Erlach's baroque Winter Riding School perpetuates all the airs and graces of a lost age. Inside, the magnificent chandeliers, the gracious decor, lend an air of theatrical unreality so that the fairytale white horses are only enlarged versions of the porcelain Lipizzaner stallions selling outside at $45–$100 as tourist souvenirs.

And what do the tourists see? An unrivalled spectacle of equine rhythm, perfection of movement and mastery of control, once designed for the pleasure, protection and efficiency of princes and warriors long ago. Behind the spectacle is some of the most rigorous training known to horse and man. Some of the bits and spurs (with shanks nine inches long) employed originally, are decidedly not for the squeamish. William Cavendish, Duke of Newcastle, credited with inventing the Cavesson, which, with his special running rein, enabled unlimited pressure to be exerted on the horse's head and mouth, broke his horses in by running them in tight circles with their necks forcibly arched in an unnaturally taut position. The Newcastle running rein is still in use and some of his short cuts still in general practice although Gruinère's classic *Ecole de Cavalerie*, published in 1733, contains the guiding principals of the training methods still obtaining in the Spanish School.

We are told that now force is out and patience in, and that it may take seven years for a horse to master the fiendishly difficult *capriole*, an exercise which when efficiently performed gives the impression that the animal is about to tear itself into two. This and similar 'acts' are learned between two pillars (which may be seen in the arena) with the horse's head immobilized by a complicated arrangement of curbs and reins. This leaves the trainers free to signal and encourage with their whips on the remainder of the animal's anatomy. Sometimes the pillars are human, a man on either side with a hand apiece for 'reminders'. What the general public sees, as in the case of the circus animal, is the finished act and not the long years of attrition and coercion that went before. In the case of the Spanish Riding School, this has been likened to ballet and the analogy is valid. The setting indoors is certainly a picturesque backcloth and the dancers as they may be called have undergone years of rigorous training in the manner of their human counterparts. But there the analogy ends — the horses have no choice and cannot quit. They form a tremendous source of revenue without needing salaries, and to any real horselover the musclebound, nature- and gravity-defying cavortings of a captive animal are not so much a beautiful as an embarrassing spectacle.

# 4

## Pets, Zoos and Animal Traffic

'I fear that our vast urban population will become so physically remote from animal life, they will cease to care about it. Eventually someone will find the animal equivalent to the plastic flower, and that will be that.'
DR DESMOND MORRIS

People keep pets for a variety of reasons, perhaps primarily for something to love and be loved by, over which to exert a kind of compassionate power, also for companionship, as a plaything for children, as a guard-dog, working dog or status symbol, and doubtless for many more. All these reasons seem superficially valid, as one tends to assume that an animal fulfilling some of these needs would be suitably cared for; but there are also a variety of reasons for *not* owning a pet which are often not taken into consideration at the time of purchase. Pets of any sort have to be planned for when it comes to going away; they have to be fed, taken out, groomed, they make a mess, cause work and trouble and they may be expensive to maintain.

Unwanted pets usually end up in an RSPCA institution. In one large RSPCA home which we visited the dogs were fed during the day and given water, but not in the evening because of the extra work involved. For the rest of the time their life alternated between many hours in their small individual cell-like kennels and the remainder out in their concrete pens where they could pace round like caged tigers or jump up and down in frantic efforts to see what was going on in the outside world and what they might be missing. Some of the pens might have a little shelter from the small trees growing by them, others had none but the walls and wire netting.

Most of the dogs are simply unwanted, one or two are 'cruelty' cases. Some have been there many months. These are the animals that have odd appearances and could not be mistaken for anything but mongrels. They may have long legs, shaggy coats, funny eyes, or big feet, and could hardly be called beautiful. But they do not suffer any less on that account.

59

Perhaps once some family bought one of them as a darling little puppy, a welcome addition to the household. But the newcomer grew up and reasons were invented why it should be sent to the home—it was too big for the council house or flat, it was jealous of the baby, it was too rough with the children (who had probably teased it), it needed too much food or exercise or attention. Then the dog, once part of a family, finds itself in an institution, never taken for walks, never allowed freedom unless someone can be found to take it in. So it passes day after day, week after week, with no variety, its only relief from tedium being the daily meal.

The cruelty cases are perhaps better off because at least they experience some kind of security at last and a cessation of man's hostility towards them, but it is not replaced by the positive family life and attention and above all the exercise that would tire them out and make the long confinement in kennels no hardship.

In the USA there are forty million dogs and cats, homeless and unwanted, and even in a country as small as Ireland, there are never less than thirty thousand homeless cats and seven thousand dogs in institutions annually, in Dublin alone. The number of unwanted dogs brought to homes in Great Britain is growing yearly, particularly from housing estates, and in new towns and service camps. In 1968, according to the RSPCA, it reached the appalling figure of 300,000. Inspectors have told us of people coming to deposit a dog with the casual remark 'Put it down, will you?' On being questioned as to their reasons, the usual answer is: 'It's got too big' or 'It's too big for the children'. Other reasons have been: 'It barks sometimes and my wife has bad nerves', or 'we just refurnished the house and my wife doesn't like the hairs all over the place'.

Above all else, dogs need companionship. Why should we subject them to solitary confinement, locked alone in houses or cars all day? Cases have been reported of owners actually shutting dogs in the boots of cars and returning hours later to find them dead. Similarly, many have no idea of how to train a dog, so that it goes through life like a convict with its only exercise to be hauled along on a short leash; or even to house-train it, so that the dog exists in a muddling insecurity between cuffs and caresses.

In Denmark it is now illegal for dogs to be permanently chained. In Britain, an RSPCA inspector can call and suggest that the dog be unchained and exercised, but if the dog is reasonably clean and fed it would be impossible to bring a cruelty case on chaining only. However, perhaps we may claim that our dog homes and destruction methods and services are far better than those of many other countries. Obviously the more primitive and poverty-stricken the country the worse the treatment to all animals, including pets. In some Eastern and Latin American countries, unwanted dogs are rounded up in the streets by the police and clubbed to death in the mockery of a dog's home. A specific case recently cited was Bogota, Colombia, where the municipality was extremely cruel to abandoned animals. The strays were brutally treated, left without food or water for several days and then put to death by beating them with sticks. In Puerto Rico, where dogs and cats roam the streets in great numbers, if there is a rabies scare, government officials spread strychnine in meat, thus destroying many pets as well as unfortunate roving strays.

On the Spanish Mediterranean island of Ibiza unwanted dogs are rounded up and hanged like malefactors. Many holiday-makers adopt the strays, feed them and make much of them; but as soon as they leave, the wretched animals are out scavenging on the streets again. In Spain itself we saved dogs from being put to death by stoning and drowning. One that we had personally adopted had to be taken to a vet for 'painless destruction', but we later discovered that it was actually put down by strychnine, this being the Spanish idea of a painless death.

In many parts of Europe, except in bigger towns, there is no one trained to carry out painless destruction, or who has the necessary drugs, and no one who can castrate pet animals, a contributing factor to the pitiful swarm of unwanted and starving dogs and cats. The end of many of these creatures, through greed and commercial gain, is death in an experimental laboratory.

In Britain too many strays, and many pets that are not strays at all, meet the same end. In 1969 Ralf William Moore pleaded guilty at the Old Bailey to receiving cats knowing that they were stolen. In Court he said: 'I buy them from blokes in pubs. I don't ask where they get them and I don't care.' Mr John Bleby, Director of the Medical Research Council's Laboratory Animal Centre, has said that at least five thousand strays or pets are used for experiments every year.

In most of the poorer countries of the world, and quite often in rural areas of Britain, cats, even those kept domestically as pets, are not fed. Many of us know of farm-houses near which there is a troupe of scraggy, mangy, stunted cats, who never get more than an already scraped-out dish to lick, and no veterinary attention, not even simple worming. If they are ill, they recover as best they can, or simply die.

The alternative to inadequate care may be care misdirected. Thus, in Europe, in order to make his pets conform to his idea of what is attractive and fashionable, man has bred in certain characteristics which are often detrimental to the health and wellbeing of the animal, however much they may delight its owner. An example is the soft palate and compressed features of the bulldog, boxer, pekingese, pomeranian and pug. The modern trend is to breed shorter and shorter noses on this type of dog, resulting in a soft and often flabby palate, which in turn gives rise to difficulty in breathing. In extreme cases the dog pants all the time, although conditions may not appear to warrant it, the eyes protrude, and, if it is at all distressed by a rise in temperature, extra exertion, or excitement, the dog may lose consciousness. This may happen to these breeds when on a car journey and can be most distressing for the owner as well as the victim. There are also, quite frequently, difficulties and respiratory troubles during whelping, and birth may have to be by Caesarian section.

In *Genetics of the Dog*, M. Burns and M. N. Fraser point out that 'examination of Bulldog skulls in the British Museum, all from dogs born prior to 1936, show that they then had longer jaws than modern Bulldogs: in the latter, selection for wide, flat upper jaws has led to the crowding of the cheek teeth and exaggerated space for the incisors.'

Dog breeders in pursuit of a show specimen and the attendant profits may inbreed to such an extent that serious abnormalities and weaknesses result. Dwarfing, spine deformities, eye-complaints, and tendencies to kidney diseases can all result from such breeding. At the other end of the scale from the bulldog types is the borzoi and the long, narrow 'aristocratic head' which is just as abnormal.

Cruel caging is another serious problem with many pets. Some time ago we adopted a rabbit from a village woman. 'You'll want the hutch as well', she said, and brought out a box two feet six inches long by twenty inches broad. The rabbit was a large, pure white Polish about five years old. We could not help remembering the RSPCA pamphlet entitled *The Backyard Prisoner* and thinking how apt was this quotation from it: 'I have no room for exercise—yet I was born to run and leap about in the open air. You call me a pet...If you can look at me and not be saddened, well, you need sympathy *almost* as much as I do, for you have lost one of the most precious things in life—the power to feel pity.'

On transfering the rabbit to a large, grassy run we noticed its claws had grown so long through lack of all exercise that they were curled over like the letter 'C'. It could sit only in discomfort and could certainly never run. We cut the horny claws with difficulty and at first the rabbit was so stiff and cramped, unused to movement, that it could not even 'bunny-hop'. So many pet rabbits live like this.

Comparable suffering is caused by the prevalent habit of keeping goldfish in a round bowl. We did it when we were children, because no one taught us any better, and they died — or rather we killed them, or lack of imagination killed them. In their natural state, in pond or stream, the light comes from above, not from the sides, glaring and unprotected; having no eyelids, they need shelter from strong light, among the filtered light and shadowed light of the weeds.

In a round bowl, too small an area of water surface is in contact with the air to provide the necessary oxygen. Our goldfish certainly died from lack of oxygen. Often at fairs and fetes, one goldfish in a plastic bag is provided as a prize. If it survives this asphyxiation, it may die of solitude, as goldfish are naturally gregarious. In fact this whole question of giving live animals as prizes, and in sales promotion schemes, to people at random (who perhaps do not want them and will not care for them adequately, and may get rid of them to totally unsuitable homes) has long been of growing concern to all interested in animal welfare.

The official magazine of the RSPCA reports that every year large numbers of people are brought to justice on charges of catching wild birds or having them in their possession or offering them for sale.

The traffic in birds also causes death to many thousands in transit. Out of a consignment of five thousand white and black Java sparrows from Indonesia, one thousand were found dead on arrival at London airport. The birds, as reported by *The Times*, 'were flown to London in eleven open-work bamboo cages for delivery to a pet store in the Midlands. Mr Neville Whittaker, Manager of the RSPCA hostel at London Airport said they were "grossly overcrowded". There were five hundred birds in each cage, with inadequate provision for feeding and water.'

Mr Trevor Scott, chief administrator for the International Society for the Protection of Animals, also expressed particular horror at the traffic in wild birds:

> An importer can bring fifty thousand into a country which protects all its own wild birds, knowing that twenty per cent will be dead before they even reach the retailer. They are so cheap that the loss doesn't matter.

The Greek tortoise, whose actual habitat is along the Mediterranean coast from Morocco to Israel, is the tortoise most commonly sold as a pet in Britain. A quarter of a million are imported annually. Despite improved air transport conditions following agitation by the RSPCA and the University Federation for Animal Welfare, many die in transit and ninety per cent will almost certainly perish during their first winter in this country. The Russian tortoise can survive cold weather better, but because it is an expert burrower, climber and 'escaper' it is unpopular with pet shops and dealers. The *Report* of the UFAW says that tortoises require expert care if they are to survive under United Kingdom conditions. In the absence of legislation, consumer resistance to the pet tortoise trade would help to relieve suffering. Another disquieting traffic is in hatchling terrapins of *pseudemys* species, which are imported annually from America. This creature is quite unsuitable for the ordinary household and is likely to die within a few weeks of purchase.

The hostel at London Airport deals with a constant flow of distressed animals. The *Observer* reported the more spectacular cases which receive publicity — three hundred squirrels, two hundred finches packed into small boxes and suffocated, and the dead lioness, crammed into a packing case smaller than herself. As a correspondent to the *Daily Telegraph* wrote on 26 October 1965, 'It is awful to contemplate what that animal must have suffered mentally and physically in that short space of time — and to think that it was meant to continue the long haul to Karachi under such conditions'. In February 1969, three hundred and eight animals and birds were found dead on arrival at London Airport, including three hyenas in metal boxes with only nail holes for ventilation. More than two thousand animals needed first aid. In September 1965, a tiger was so distressed on arrival at London airport that it had to be given heart and lung stimulants in an attempt to save its life.

The transport of live animals and animal flight insurance is a growing business. One company faced a claim of ten thousand pounds for two gorillas which froze to death on a flight. In another instance an aardvark travelled from Ethiopia to Philadelphia, USA. There was nobody to meet this 400-pound animal when the plane landed at Philadelphia, so it sat at the airport for many hours, caught cold and died, because the zoo had not been notified of its arrival time.

*The Guardian* of 23 July 1966 reported that three cigarette crates which arrived at London airport aboard a Japan Airlines plane from Hong Kong were found to contain twenty squirrels. Each was in a wire cage, shaped like a Dutch cheese, twelve inches across and six inches deep. None had food or water and two were dead. The cages appeared to have been designed as treadmills turning on their axes.

64

The result of scientific experiment on living animals. Here the head of a dog has been grafted on to the neck of another dog. (*Pixfeatures*)

Battery hens, who are born, live and die in these conditions. (*Jurg Harry Meyer*)

On the trail of an otter. The hunt will culminate in the seemingly needless death of the animal. (*Michael Ward*)

The RSPCA says it might be illegal to keep squirrels permanently in such cages in Britain. The airlines certainly accept boxes which do not conform to the British standard. Mr Neville Whittaker, the manager of the RSPCA hostel, said 'It is nothing to put an animal in a box a foot shorter than itself'. Mr Trevor Scott, chief administrator of the RSPCA, said:

> Crates are often used more than once. One turned up at London Airport labelled 'Baby Elephant, Maintain at 75 degrees F'. It turned out to be a Shetland pony. The Society has also suggested that live animals be specially designated cargo so that aircrew and airport staff are aware that animals are being carried – not always the case at present – and that an aircraft should carry a humane killer. A horse that went berserk over the Atlantic had to be beaten to death.

Gavin Maxwell in *Ring of Bright Water* described how he ordered two otters to be sent by air. Anxious to meet them he phoned the dealer responsible for importing them but was told that they were not ready for collection. When he and a friend arrived before the appointed hour he found 'the crate was standing still unopened as it had stood since the small hours of the morning. The two occupants were weak and shivering, standing in their own dung and urine. Mine died the next day in the zoo hospital, my friend's in his wife's lap where she had sat up all night trying to coax life into the pathetic creature.' Gavin Maxwell asks if we are justified in exporting exotic pets to suffer like this. But even since he wrote, the trend is increasing and suffering escalates.

The trade in exotic animals as pets is undoubtedly growing. Zoos, circuses, private menageries and performing animal films do much to popularize this cult, which inflicts totally unnecessary misery on creatures in unsuitable surroundings and conditions.

Gerald Durrell, in the *Radio Times* of 12 October 1967, described all the problems involved in caging, feeding and doctoring exotic animals, even in a well-run zoo; so it is not surprising that the purchasers of such 'pets', without facilities and with little conception of what is involved, are inundating Regent's Park and Whipsnade zoos with pleas to take them off their hands, because they simply cannot cope. Yet the numbers imported are ever growing. Exotic animals have, in fact, become one more gimmick, with reptiles and amphibians growing increasingly popular. Such extremes did this trend reach in the United States, that snakes, alligators and baby crocodiles were flushed down lavatories and drains because they had become unmanageable. In the sewer systems of some cities they grew to full size, so that sewer-workers could no longer venture down until the animals had been destroyed.

Probably monkeys, entirely cut off from their natural environment, are among the worst sufferers, whether in pet shops, unsuitable zoo conditions, or private ownership. One can see cages of newly-arrived baby monkeys clinging pathetically together, taken far too young from their mothers, in the back quarters of some pet-shops; and one hears about cases of monkeys found frozen to death for lack of appropriate heating in smaller zoos and of humane benefactors installing heating at their own expense in others.

Vera Ryder, in *Living with Monkeys*, describes the arrival at her monkey-home of a young Capucin from Cornwall.

> According to reports he was in a very poor state. They were keeping it in a parrot cage, and there appeared to be something wrong with its legs...But I hadn't bargained for the sight which met my eyes when I lifted the lid of the box in which it had travelled, and gazed down upon quite the most dreadful and pitiful object I had ever seen. There on the straw lay an exact replica of one of the worst RSPCA advertisements you can imagine—a tiny bag of bones with a completely hairless tail, the tip hanging by a thread, enormous frightened eyes and trembling claw-like hands. When I had lifted out the pathetic scrap with the utmost care in case something broke, I saw that the legs were doubled beneath the body in the most curious shape. The little creature could hardly move, much less sit or stand, and cried out with every movement. Due to lack of calcium the legs, which had been broken in at least three places, had failed to mend and were just a series of right-angles. Looking at that fragile wreck lying on its side on the hay, I was filled with rage that because of man's cruel indifference and ignorance a living creature should have been brought to such a state. It was now up to me to try to restore it to some semblance of a monkey.

*Life* magazine in November 1968 contained an article entitled 'The shame of the Naked Cage' which stated that the wild animal trade is such a flourishing business that last year the United States alone imported more than twenty-eight million live creatures—seventy-five thousand of them mammals. Relatively few of these were actually destined for the public zoos and aquariums in the country. The vast majority, according to *Life*, went to pet shops. The magazine also reported that for $2,000 the affluent animal fancier can, *by mail order*, purchase a dangerously playful baby jaguar. The article went on to state that the most wasteful aspect of this traffic was the mortality rate: for every animal that survived the ordeal of capture (many animals died simply from the shock of being captured) and shipping, countless others have died.

The Catholic Study Circle for Animal Welfare reported an extensive illegal trade in orang-utans, centred at Singapore, where one specimen will fetch anything between five hundred and nine hundred pounds. Zoos are among the main buyers, and the suppliers are usually soldiers, sailors and employees of airlines.

Soldiers and natives kill orang-utan mothers, as the babies then attach themselves to the murderers. The wife of Sarawak's Zoo curator has inaugurated a rescue service, and when illegal traders can be caught the baby orang-utans are re-trained for life in the jungle, since this species of ape is in grave danger of extinction.

Comparatively little is known of the effect on wild animals of the frustration, loneliness and deprivation of vital instinctual life suffered by captives in zoos; so many species never breed, or even mate, (as to date the pandas An-An and Chi-Chi have not mated) and others mysteriously die off in captivity. Alice, the London Zoo's only walrus, died late in 1967 of internal haemorrhage, although she was in perfect health on arrival from Russia the previous December.

Recently two polar bear cubs died within hours of each other at the menagerie being held at the Kelvin Hall in Glasgow from a stress condition associated with so much travelling and handling, as the post-mortem examination disclosed. They were owned by Associated Pleasure Parks and were on loan to Glasgow Corporation for the city's annual carnival.

Vernon Reynolds, in his field study of the wild chimpanzees in an African forest, for which he was awarded a University of London post-graduate scholarship, writes of apes in captivity:

> What hypocrisy in a people professing to love of animals and knowing of the remarkable intelligence and emotional make-up of the chimpanzee, to condemn him to life imprisonment with solitary confinement, for no fault of his own.

He is familiar with the arguments about space and housing being expensive; but he truly says that there are no half-measures without cruelty, and that while better accommodation is on the drawing board, the chimps are best left in the jungle.

Apart from the rare specialized zoo, such as the Woolly Monkey Colony at Looe in Cornwall, where the monkeys are able to live in a natural environment, even the best zoos fail to allow instinctual patterns to proceed unhampered. In an article in *Life* magazine, entitled 'Must we have Zoos? Yes, but...' Desmond Morris, Curator of Mammals at London Zoo and world-famed zoologist, says:

67

There is something biologically immoral about keeping animals in enclosures where their behaviour patterns, which have taken millions of years to evolve, can find no expression. Animals do not live by nutrition alone...Everywhere you turn in old-fashioned zoos, behaviour starvation faces you. Nesting, bed-making, bathing, playing, scent-making, sleeping, wallowing, defecating, territorial patrolling, displaying, social grouping—all these patterns, which may seem so trivial, so easily reducible to minimal expression, are being frustrated and prevented from finding full behavioural outlet.

Weaverbirds should be allowed to weave, beavers to build dams, apes to construct beds, elephants to bathe, bowerbirds to erect bowers, young chimps to swing and play, deer to form mud wallows, wolves to scent posts and bears to climb trees. Above all, social species must be allowed to live in natural social groups of the correct size and composition and not always in neat pairs, as if they were candidates for some ludicrous Noah's Ark, or, worse still, singly, in a painful solitary confinement.

# 5

# *Hunting with Hounds*

'There is in a passion for hunting, something deeply implanted in the human breast.'
CHARLES DICKENS

The subject of hunting game with the aid of hounds arouses strong emotions of both love and hate. One only has to think of Surtees, but the opposition is equally enthusiastic. Addison, born in 1672, could declare unequivocally that 'Hunting is no fit pastime for a thinking man.' And Dr Johnson added: 'It is very strange and very melancholy that the paucity of human pleasures should ever persuade us to call hunting one of them.' There followed Cowper's indictment of 'detested sport that owes its pleasures to another's pain'.

These critics of blood-sports lived in a century when the 'paucity of human pleasures' turned the idle rich to hunting as a matter of course. Today, leisure and affluence are offered a wide range of pursuits and pastimes, from motor racing to ten-pin bowling, from dinghy-sailing to gliding, from mountaineering to pot-holing, which do not derive their thrills from the lethal chase of a relatively defenceless animal. Yet the number of hunt clubs grows, in spite of all these other outlets for skill and energy and daring. Perhaps this is because our tradition of sport still runs true to Pope's description of how we influence children:

> One of the first pleasures we allow them is the license of inflicting pain on poor animals. Almost as soon as they are sensible what life is, ourselves, we make it our sport to take it from other creatures.

Thomas Moore went further with his injunction:

> Thou shouldst rather be moved to pity to see a silly, innocent hare murdered of a dog, the weaker of the stronger, the fearful of the fierce.

Today, opponents of hunting are frequently told by those whose sports they criticize that they have no right to complain or level charges of cruelty while they themselves eat meat. We have not become nationally converted to vegetarianism, yet we no longer practise bull and bear baiting.

Hunting with hounds in Britain is not confined to the landed classes. Indeed they may very well opt out of their traditional 'duty' in this respect, being too busy attending to the farming of their shrinking estates or opening up their ancient homes to the public. Nowadays a fair sprinkling of business and professional men support the hunt, seeking relaxation and a complete change from commerce in the thrill and absorption of the chase. Those not born into the squirearchy may nonetheless aim at this desirable image, fostered while young by their parents and by some types of educational upbringing.

Hunting needs an influx of money as the cost of maintaining hunt establishments rises. To encourage this kind of new support an enterprising Cotswold horse dealer in 1956 advertised a scheme to provide 'accommodation, a suitable mount and full tuition in hunting etiquette for an all-in fee of twelve guineas per day'. But one hunting gentleman was reported as finding this 'most objectionable', adding 'he won't get away with it, we don't want to encourage outsiders'. Under the headline 'Into Sport by the Backdoor' the promoter insisted that it was a confidential service and that no one would know that the people staying with him 'were not genuine hunting people with their own horses and equipment'.

We learned first-hand of one outsider who certainly was 'most objectionable'. A *nouveau riche* from the West Midlands, he was welcomed by the local hunt because he had ample means and leisure. But he had little experience of horses and a filthy temper. Regardless of cost, he bought Irish bloodstock, and one of his more mettlesome mounts, possibly upset at the manner in which it was being ridden, bolted with him along the edge of a fearsome quarry, terrifying its rider. It was near the end of the day, and when the horse had been brought under control again its owner ordered his groom to hold it while he meted out punishment for the fright it had given him. In bloodsports as in war there is nothing so merciless as the man who has just got over the fright of his life and is now in a position to avenge himself on the cause of it. He beat the animal with the handle of his heavy riding crop, in the course of the punishment beating out both its eyes, according to our friend who witnessed the incident. He tried to stop the worst of the thrashing too late, and pointed out that there were ladies present who were on the verge of weeping and who were begging him to desist.

We asked our friend if the man was reported to the RSPCA or police and he replied, 'Good gracious, no, we kept it to ourselves for the sake of the hunt, but the fellow was never asked to any of our houses again.'

A decade or so later it is possible that one of the bystanders would have reported the incident. It is even possible although not very likely that the groom might have given evidence and so lost his job. But it takes an exceptional employee, whether of the hunt, farm, racetrack or circus, to take such a self-destroying step, and mostly they have been so indoctrinated by the attitudes surrounding their livelihood that such a course would hardly occur to them.

Often the backbone of any hunting fraternity are Service people and it is not for nothing that Surtees described hunting as 'The sport of kings, the image of war without its *guilt* and only five and twenty per cent of its dangers'.

In many respects, hunting is both a rehearsal and a substitute for war, and more than one officer had led his men 'into battle' with a hunting horn. In the hunting field the officer commands a pack of hounds rather than men, and the 'enemy', while cunning and swift, may stand at bay but is never a real threat to the opposing forces. Strategy and planning is involved, and cries of 'kill 'im' may sound warlike enough, but there *is* only a very small percentage of danger, even when all the broken legs and collarbones are taken into account. There are casualties among the horses occasionally, and hounds themselves are sometimes electrocuted on railway lines, mowed down by trains, hit by cars whose drivers see them too late, or even suffocated in their overcrowded, often ill-ventilated, transports. Sometimes they are neglected in kennels to the point of an RSPCA prosecution, which happened in the West Country in the early fifties.

At one hunt we noted forty hounds and two terriers packed into one van with only rear door ventilation. They were literally on top of one another and had travelled fifty miles to the meet under these conditions. The day was warm, one terrier looked considerably the worse for wear, and we reflected that any commercial dog-breeder transporting animals in this manner would be subject to enquiry and most probably prosecution. But the hunts are a law unto themselves, and although their business is killing wild life no one ever seems to question their fitness to deal with other animals, the horses and hounds.

If the tough image of war is reflected by the service personnel who hunt, it is paradoxical that British forces in West Germany, where hunting as we know it is illegal, have organized a most successful drag-hunt. The Wessex Pack began as fox-hounds but settled down to being a drag-pack very well. *Horse and Hound* stated that 'contrary to gloomy prophecies, hounds spoke well to the aniseed line throughout the season, possibly because they always "killed" a sandbag of raw meat at the end of the line.'

In the Netherlands, too, hunting has been illegal since the beginning of the century. The Royal Dutch Hunt Society, founded in 1919, organizes 'slip hunts', their hounds following an artificially plotted course with regularly placed scent which ensures a good run, without either killing an animal or damaging farmland or property.

If this kind of hunting were adopted in Britain, many heated arguments and subsequent court cases for trespass and damage would be avoided. In addition, humane people would be satisfied because a sentient creature was no longer being used as a sporting accessory, and the complex of country economics dependent on the sport would not be affected, as the farrier, saddler, horse transport agents and the rest would be if hunting were suddenly stopped entirely.

Drag-hunting might even bring new recruits to the sport from those few pony-club members who still resist indoctrination into a sport which involves killing. At present such children and their parents appear to be in a minority. The horsemanship is always stressed, while the last thing emphasized or even mentioned is the 'kill'. If the critics of hunting bring up the state of the fox or other quarry they will be told that the field can have many hunts without ever witnessing the kill. Often in conversation with sportsmen the impression is subtly conveyed that it is not done to mention the plight of the quarry at all. Cruelty, suffering, and fear are dirty words. It is the hunt which is important. The kill hardly matters at all.

The National Society for the Abolition of Cruel Sports, advocating drag-hunting, points out that a live quarry adds nothing to the hunt, and may make a day's hunt consist of milling about from one check point to another. This is perfectly true. Much time is spent in the hunting field just waiting for a fox to break cover or for something to happen. The quarry can also lead hounds to a motorway, a railway line or over a cliff, or cause damage to farming or private interests, all of which can be avoided by a carefully laid drag.

But diehard hunting enthusiasts argue that the drag is only a substitute, although it could be the complete answer to their critics. They could still enjoy the wildly exhilarating crosscountry chase, but not at the expense of an animal's exhaustion, terror and death.

There have always been those who have questioned the right of the

hunting fraternity to inflict cruelty in the name of sport. To defend
their traditions and to consolidate their position, the British Field
Sports Society was formed in 1930. We have known fox-hunters who
criticized stag and otter hunting, and even some who saw no pleasure
in coursing, but they closed their ranks by joining the British Field
Sports Society, for to defend one was to defend all, and to criticize one
branch of blood sports might endanger all. After the Second World
War, criticism mounted. It seemed as though the general public had
seen enough violence and cruelty, and under the Labour government a
bill was brought to outlaw hunting. The British Field Sports Society
had a membership of 36,230 at the time, the two main anti-hunt
societies about 12,000 paid-up members between them, but in addition to this there was the large body of public opinion which, while not
actually joining any society, revealed in letters to the press that it was
against hunting.

The bill was defeated, although the speeches for it cut right across
party politics, and it looked as though there might be some chance of
success in stopping the hunting of deer, at least. The attempt to curb
their cherished and traditional sports caused the British Field Sports
Society to overhaul their public image, and their public relations
officer laid down a code of conduct, particularly in dealing with the
press:

> Some journalists are slightly embarrassed and ill at ease with hunting
> people, but if you are short with them they may try to assert them-
> selves—you may think it a good idea to send the Editor a couple of
> tickets for the Hunt Ball. Do not enter into discussion on cruelty, show
> you are human and treat the other people as if they are human.
>
> When writing hunting reports for your local paper or the sporting
> press it is wise to avoid stressing details which may provide anti-hunting
> organizations with ammunition to attack field sports. Reports should be
> restricted to description of the country hunted over, with as much detail
> as you like of hound work, but avoid stressing details of the kill—i.e.
> 'hounds killing their dead beat fox' 'the digging out of a fox' and
> 'hounds deserving their taste of blood' the wisest expression to use is
> that a fox was 'accounted for'. Try to avoid the term 'blood sports',
> this was coined by the anti-hunt organizations to conjure up a gory
> picture. *Field sports* is more suitable.

But is it? To the layman, 'field sports' may well conjure up pastimes
like archery or crosscountry running or even ball games! The
euphemism is obviously intentional and misleading, on a par with
'culling' for killing. But the hunting controversy was at last out in the
open. With fewer tenant farmers and hunting landlords, even the

agricultural press began to print as many letters criticizing hunting as defending it.

In 1948 one of the authors sent a reasonable letter to a country journal claiming the biggest circulation in the south and west of England. In it she suggested that, with most poultry penned up, the fox was not the unmitigated evil hunting people would suggest, and that in fact with its enormous appetite for small rodents it did as much good as harm. Furthermore, she concluded that we preferred the fox to the hunt and its followers, and that as foxes were encouraged to breed in artificial earths in a nearby cover, no one could claim that hunting was a method of controlling the fox population.

The editor, a personal friend, refused to publish this letter, although he said he absolutely agreed with it, commenting that if he printed it, he would have a hornets' nest about his ears. Twenty years later the son of this editor, having succeeded to his father's chair, could allow more space in his columns to the pros and cons of hunting than almost any other subject.

For if the British Field Sports Society have organized their propaganda, the opponents of hunting have also become more articulate, and this vexed question has been debated in the correspondence columns of many newspapers and magazines and on radio and television. Even tenants of sporting landlords have been known to enter the lists, a state of affairs unthinkable a couple of decades ago.

But a subtle blow was struck for hunting by the Committee of Enquiry set up in 1951 after the failure of the anti-hunting bill. No anti-hunt society was represented on this committee, which was composed almost entirely of sporting interests in one form or another. The finding of the Scott Henderson committee was, briefly that hunting was the most humane form of control at present and that little cruelty was involved, although perhaps otter hunting involved more suffering than other forms of sport. These findings were largely foreseen by the cynical as a sop to public opinion and therefore a block to future progress or reform. It is interesting to note that while otter hunting was admittedly causing suffering there was no move made to limit it, even on the grounds that numbers were insufficient to be of 'pest' proportions. Fifteen years later otter numbers were low enough to cause nation-wide concern and lead naturalists to state that the otter might well be on the way to extinction. In this respect the otter differs from the other main quarries, fox, deer, and hare, and so will be dealt with in a separate chapter.

74

Let us take the fox first, because when most people refer to hunting it is the image of a pack of fox-hounds pursuing a small reddish animal, followed by men and women in 'pink' coats on horseback that is conjured up.

Fox-hunting is a comparatively recent innovation, however; up to the eighteenth century the fox was vermin and not to be classed with game worthy of the chase.

In Britain there are just over two hundred packs of fox-hounds meeting several times a week during the season, from November to March. In 1960 the Ministry of Agriculture gave the figure of foxes killed by hunts at 21,000 for thirteen months, which is about 19,000 in a year, discounting those that are trapped, snared, shot, killed on the roads or which die a natural death.

At this rate the fox population might soon be extinct, but to ensure a steady supply for sport and as few blank days as possible, they are encouraged to breed. Artificial earths are provided in suitable covers for the vixen to make her home, and in wild, often unhunted districts, cubs are captured and taken to sporting areas to keep up the supply.

A letter to *The Times* in 1967 stated that the writer, while out walking, saw a rifled fox earth: 'We were told the vixen might return to rear the cubs, but when we returned next day we saw seven dead or dying cubs who had tried to eat earth in their hunger and had bitten through their tongues.' These cubs could easily have been destroyed in the first place.

When challenged on the cruelty issue, hunting people will point to the fox's chance of escape, which they put as high as fifty-fifty. But actually the fox that eludes hounds at the end of the day may still not get off scot-free. H. Wentworth Day, the sporting writer, describes a Quorn incident:

> They had lost a fox in a drain several times that season, so the Master had the drain opened up; inside they found the skeletons of no fewer than ten foxes; all no doubt had died as the result of crawling into a damp drain when they were overheated, for in spite of their tremendous courage, tenacity and wiry energy, foxes are highly nervous, sensitive animals.

The same theme is echoed by Mortimer Batten in *British Wild Animals*:

> Many a good fox who has fooled and baffled the hounds and given them a glorious run has won his freedom at the cost of constitutional fitness. Emerging at length from his sanctuary after a rest of many hours, he is no longer the wonderful running machine that he was

75

when hounds took up his scent, but is now a broken creature, lungs gone, heart gone, merely a physical wreck.

It is here, surely, in the chase and even the 'escape' that the charge of cruelty must be met, not just in the kill or the 'accounting for'.

Captain Robert Churchward, after being a joint master of the South Shropshire Foxhounds and appearing in the film of Mary Webb's *Gone to Earth*, wrote: 'It is time everyone knew something that it has taken me over forty years to learn—that fox hunting is organized torture leading to murder.' In his book, *A Master of Hounds Speaks*, he particularly stresses the cruelty latent in 'cubbing' when young hounds are taught their work against inexperienced foxcubs.

> The pups, lacking the experience of older hounds, were not quite sure how to deal with the cub. They bit it and were bitten back. They treated it both as something to kill and something to play with. There was a sordid scuffle in which fur, flesh and blood flew in all directions.

Every season the press comes out with bad 'incidents', hounds that over-run a garden and kill a pet cat by mistake, foxes torn to pieces in some school playground in full sight of the children, spent foxes dug out or pulled from the branch of a tree refuge and thrown to hounds. The nature of hunting with its unpredictable conditions, makes such incidents probable, but a drag-hunt would eliminate them. It might, however, be argued that a drag-hunt would not keep foxes down. The RSPCA, while opposed to the hunting of any animal for sport, does not press for legislation against fox-hunting because the alternatives may present more cruelty, but the Society has offered a reward of £1,000 for a humane and effective means of fox control. A referendum taken in 1968 showed an overwhelming majority of members were against hunting, but as the British Field Sports Society supports the RSPCA as a matter of policy it would mean an important split in membership if the RSPCA gave way to public opinion on this question.

But, as farmers, we have come to the conclusion that hunting perpetuates cruelty in no uncertain way. Foxes can be shot quite easily. They have recognized habits, times and routes. Shooting is cruel only when the marksmanship is bad: hunting causes suffering always, even when the quarry escapes. Fox numbers would be kept to reasonable proportions if hunts did not demand a large population for sporting purposes. Furthermore, when considering farming interests, it is the hunted fox, no longer the fit creature he once was, who will take the easy meal offered by the farmyard. An Exmoor clergyman who had a fox killed by hounds in his churchyard has suggested to us that foxes habitually hunted know that they are in perpetual danger and that it is vital for them not to be hungry. The fact of being hunted also makes them more vicious hunters themselves. One must remember that hunting is not a natural hazard for foxes. Dogs could be driven mad by such cruelty; what of the fox?

It is an interesting theory and one which our own experience bore out. We did not allow any of the hunts on our two hundred acres and several neighbouring farmers joined us in forming a hunt-free area. Our barns were kept largely free of rats and mice. During the bitter winter of 1963-4 woodpigeons were taken, but we had no trouble from our foxes, except that if we buried the carcase of a 'casualty' hen or a piglet which the sow had lain on, it would be dug up.

When it comes to deer-hunting, the problems are different. Unlike the fox, who is omnivorous and a scavenger, deer will eat growing crops. In severe weather and if their numbers warrant it they will invade farmland bordering their wild habitat. They can be shot, but with powerful rifles and telescopic sights there is little challenge to a true sportsman. In the Highlands of Scotland and elsewhere deer are killed in this way, usually efficiently and humanely. In 1963 a Protection of Deer Act was passed, aimed largely at protecting deer from gangs of poachers who were finding the sale of venison very lucrative.

This Act, concerned with some protection of deer, has been called the sportsman's charter by the anti-hunting faction, and certainly it did not aim in any way to protect the hunted deer of Exmoor. The notorious Devon and Somerset staghounds are often in the news. This is partly because they operate in an area now readily accessible to holiday-makers and at a time of year, commencing with the third week in August, when plenty of people are at hand to witness their activities. Many a holiday-maker thrilled to find a bit of tradition on show has accidentally seen the less happy side of the hunted stag or hind and become overnight an anti-bloodsport convert.

A fox can escape down a hole or a drain, if he is lucky, but there is no such escape possible for a large animal like a stag. He is run until failing lungs and stiffening muscles bring him to bay. If hounds are well ahead of the field, as often happens in wild and difficult terrain the dogs may worry him and inflict serious wounds before the huntsman can come up with them and deliver the *coup de grâce*.

Exhausted hunted stags sometimes seek sanctuary in built-up areas and then the 'bad incidents' get into the newspapers. Recently a spent stag was cornered in a Barnstaple factory yard and there despatched to the cry of 'butchering, not sport!' A tired stag with stiffening limbs finds it increasingly hard to jump obstacles, and so we have the spectacle of a large creature impaled on the railings of a school playground while someone is sent for a gun to finish it off.

Seeking a last chance to escape the hounds who are closing in, deer will try to leap barbed wire or stone walls, will swim rivers or take to the sea. No one who has seen an exhausted stag, its tongue lolling, flank heaving, can suppose it is not terrified and knows it is running for its life. Hinds have been known to be hunted with calf at foot and carrying young. The Devon and Somerset Staghounds hunt three times a week from the end of August to April; the present master reckons he has killed more than one thousand stags himself. The death of a large deer is a messy business and the comparison with butchering is apt. A fox may disappear beneath hounds in a flurry of fur and snapping bone, but the death of a stag or hind can be long-drawn out and bloody, distressing to all but the dedicated hunter.

The hunting of the hare is the next subject of this chapter. This animal, in addition to being coursed by greyhounds or whippets or any other fleet-footed dog, and being chased by packs of beagles and followers on foot, is also hunted by packs accompanied by a mounted 'field' and these are known as harriers. Once the hare was the important quarry, next the stag, while the fox was only vermin. This may have been because, although sport was important to country life, so were the products of the kill. Deer and hare were good food, but Oscar Wilde's phrase, 'the unspeakable in pursuit of the uneatable' has always been an apt description of fox-hunting.

At one time during the thirties, at least one West Country pack grew short of hares. When the hunted population grew to a dangerously low level, a sporting farmer who was a member of the local harriers was entrusted with the task of importing hares from districts where they were more plentiful and providing good living and breeding-conditions for them on his farm. It was made pretty clear that his future tenancy and local goodwill depended on his having a good supply of hares ready for sport. They were kept literally in clover in a wired-in field against the day of the chase. At his death, his obituary noted that this very 'sporting' farmer had always done his duty by the local hunt, of which he was a keen member. The next generation on the farm, although brought up to hunt both hare and fox, declined to set the screams of 'puss' or the terrified snarl of the spent fox in the scales against personal pleasure and took up sailing instead.

Lower in the social scale, after the harriers, comes beagling. Because beagling is done on foot, it is popular with public schools and service establishments such as Dartmouth Naval College and it offers exercise and an introduction into bloodsports for little outlay. Beagles are a special type of hound, about fourteen inches high, bred for stamina. They are delightful dogs and make excellent pets. Their quarry is the hare, fleet of foot but no match for the dogs and often so terrified that it does not make any real attempt to get away.

Beagles are not the only enemy that 'puss' has to contend with, since greyhounds have also taken up the chase. In the towns it has been thought that urban sensibilities required a mechanical hare at racing tracks. In the coursing field, the live animal is used. There are about twenty-five coursing clubs in Great Britain, which between them hold about ninety meetings each season, of which the Waterloo Cup held on Lord Sefton's estate is the most notable.

Increasing pressure has been brought to bear by the humane societies to abolish this particular form of sport where the hare often ends up as a living rope in a greyhound tug of war. Mr Edward Whitley, a member of the RSPCA Council reporting on the Waterloo meeting in a letter to the *Observer*, wrote:

— If it was known what goes on at these meetings there would be a widespread call for the sport to be made illegal. On the first day of the 1964 meeting I witnessed twenty-two *tugs of war* out of twenty-four kills. One took place a few yards from where I was standing and the hare screamed loudly for fourteen seconds, timed by my stopwatch. In 1965 a veterinary surgeon timed a series of such living tugs of war, one of them lasting for over one and a half minutes. No wonder the organizers of this event will not allow photographs or films to be taken while coursing is in progress. If anyone chased a cat or a dog in the way that these hares are chased, he would be liable to prosecution.

Bills to abolish hare coursing have been brought before Parliament but have been talked out. Mr Eric Heffer, MP for Walton, reintroduced his 1967 bill in the following year, after a public opinion poll had indicated that 75 per cent thought the government should make time for the bill, and that 77 per cent of the population disapproved of live hare coursing and only 12 per cent approved. Indignation against this sport was fanned by press reports and revelations that hares were 'bagged' and turned out on strange territory to run for their lives. One Waterloo Cup witness, backing Heffer's bill, wrote: 'I saw forty-four hares die in agony and heard their pitiful screams as they were ripped apart by greyhounds.' The bill was talked out. The Waterloo Cup is a great financial success and is still legal.

But hunting with dogs is obviously a spectacle that modern man enjoys as much as his predecessor did. In Scott's *Guy Mannering*, Captain Brown exclaims: 'An otter hunt the next day and a badger baiting the day after consumed the time merrily.'

And in our times, in *The Field* in 1965 a letter appeared from which the following is an extract:

> I started by cubbing with the Exmoor foxhounds who met at Malmsmead. After they had killed a fox in Badgeworthy Water I set off for Winsford Hill where I arrived in time to see the Devon and Somerset Staghounds rouse a well grown big-bodied stag from Red Cleeve—I was fortunate enough to be present when the deer was taken in the Barle, just above Marsh bridge. The stag had an unusual head with brow, tray and three and with a third straight horn on the offside with three atop. Leaving the staghounds I picked up the Culmstock Otter Hounds as they were drawing down the Aville below Knowle on a fresh drag. Just after Kitswell, hounds marked under an old weir and they accounted for a fifteen pound bitch otter. So in the space of *one day* I had hunted with three different types of packs and been present at the kill of each of their quarry, an experience not easy to achieve and only possible in that hunter's paradise Exmoor.

# 6

## Badgers and Otters

'A poor little beast desperately fighting for its life against murderous crowds of dogs and men.'
J. L. KIPLING

In Britain, at least, both otter and badger occupy distinct positions in the field of blood sports. Champions of hunting can always point to the fact that their quarry is to some extent preserved for the purposes of sport, and certainly, in spite of the numbers killed, there is no shortage (except with local and temporary fluctuations) of fox, deer, or hare, in the areas where they are hunted.

Not so much is known about otter hunts or badger digs (or baits) by the general public. It would be difficult to ignore a fox-hunt in full cry and full view, even if we were not well acquainted with the general appearance of the sport from countless illustrations and Christmas cards, calendars and table-mats. But few people, apart from the sports-men themselves, have much idea of what goes on at an otter hunt, nor of the way in which badgers are used for sport. We have met people who have lived in the country all their lives but have never seen an otter and know nothing about the nature of badgers, although they may have seen a dead one killed by a car on the roads at night.

Both beasts have a great deal to recommend them and on balance do more good than harm, both are the victims of prejudice, and both have been in the news very much of recent years as naturalists and con-servationists have worked to secure some degree of protection for them. And there the similarity ends, for the otter is hunted with all the ritual of an ancient blood sport, while the badger is persecuted by any countryman (sometimes aided by townsmen) who fancies a little 'fun'.

In Britain the otter's only real enemy is the hunt, and the fact that he is fast vanishing from our rivers and may be in danger of extinction can be attributed to the hunters. He may be a test case for the necessity of laws to enforce conservation. As the otter's case is more precarious than the badger's, we will begin with him.

The British otter (*lutra Lutra*) is, according to official circles, suffering a 'mysterious decline'. The decline is not so mysterious when one considers that there are sometimes as many as thirty-two meets of otter hounds in one week throughout the hunting season from April to October.

While it is true that increasing urbanization and the pollution of rivers have not helped the otter population, and that damage by escaped wild mink may be laid at the otter's door, bringing retaliation from keepers and poultry-farmers, it must also be true that killing otters for sport is unlikely to increase their numbers.

Apart from the fact that there is no close season and that bitch otters may be hunted and killed while pregnant or caring for litters, otters will not breed unless assured of security and seclusion. The constant disturbance by hounds and humans into their territory must have some effect on the habits of the otter population. On our southern rivers, some streams are hunted several times weekly for the entire season, giving wild life little opportunity for that essential peace and security in which to breed.

The Hunting Appointments entry in *Horse and Hound* give particulars of summer meets of thirteen different otter hound packs, meeting two or three times (and in one case four times) each week, throughout the season. In more northerly counties, the Lake District and Border country, there may be more opportunity for hunted beasts to find alternative breeding sites, but in the increasingly industrialized and overpopulated south, the dice is loaded heavily against them. Conservation rather than sport should be the first consideration when dealing with such a fascinating and relatively harmless mammal, which is not classified as an agricultural 'pest'.

After more than twenty years' experience of otter hunts it seems to us that, of all blood sports, otter-hunting is the least defensible. Even the opponents of fox-hunting can, with a little imagination, appreciate the thrill of riding to hounds, of following scent over country and being literally carried away by the excitement of the chase. The field may also go out many times without actually seeing the kill, and if they wish to justify their particular form of sport they can claim that it is healthy exercise and improves the breed of horses, gives work to saddlers and farriers and keeps down (ostensibly) an agricultural pest.

None of these lines of defence applies to otter-hunting. Those who follow otter hounds can keep up with the pack and if there is a kill are not likely to miss it. The kill can be much more long-drawn-out and brutal than in the case of the fox. The otter is lithe, slippery and has a thick layer of fat which makes it difficult for hounds to deliver the *coup de grâce*. The quarry, once marked, is largely confined to a comparatively small stretch of country, and the field have only to walk a few paces to cut off the swimming otter. They may also make detours across bridges, or take Landrovers along drove-roads to head off their quarry, who is meanwhile swimming the circuitous loops of his natural element, the river. In many ways the dice are more heavily loaded against the hunted otter than against any other quarry. At the same time, the action of setting out to kill him is more calculated and cold-blooded than is any involved in riding to hounds.

The otter is one of the most exciting and interesting of our remaining British mammals. The Ministry of Agriculture and Fisheries have never claimed that it is classified officially as a pest. The otter fishes for its food but it has been proved that it does not always take the fish which the angler values most and in fact eats a large number of eels which prey on fish spawn, and which would thereby reduce the numbers of the fisherman's catch. A sure way to improve the trout fishing in any river is to reduce the number of eels, and this is exactly what the otter does.

It is interesting to note that in the preface to *Predatory Mammals in Britain*, issued under the joint auspices of the Council for Nature and the British Field Sport Society, Professor H. R. Hewer, OBE, writes: 'damage should be assessed in relation to other possibly beneficial activities. An example is the varied diet of the otter, on balance helpful to fishing interests.' The otter does not interfere with farm livestock or bother the farmer in any way. He will eat frogs (another enemy of fish spawn), diseased fish, worms, beetles, freshwater crayfish, and small rodents. None of this really interferes with man, who has yet contrived to bring otter numbers so low that fears have been expressed about possible survival. The World Wildlife Fund has asked the Mammal Society to undertake an urgent survey of the otter situation. Mr Peter Scott is quoted as saying: 'There has been a catastrophic decline of the otter in some areas'. This is endorsed by Mr David Newman of the Scientific Committee of the Brecknock Naturalists Trust who reports that the otter population has been declining for ten years.

Wales with its national parks, its many rivers and huge complex of reservoirs and catchment areas, has long been an otter stronghold, but it is also well-hunted. Mr Newman is quoted as having found only two holts containing young in his area that season. He reported that the water was low, and that the Hawkstone Hunt's hounds 'would be able to get into the holts easily'.

Contributing to the decline is the fact that otters are hunted all through their breeding season, when the cubs are either killed by hounds, drowned in trying to escape, or left to starve when the bitch is hunted and killed; for young otters are particularly helpless at first and are suckled for two months. They have to be taught both to swim and to fend for themselves, and even after they are weaned, the dog-otter in particular will bring back food to the holt for his dependent family. When this family life is broken up by the hunt, more than just the slaughtered otter may prove to be the victim.

Pregnant otters are also hunted. In theory the hunts prefer to leave such otters to provide sport for another day. In practice it is not always possible to tell whether a bitch is pregnant while she is still partly submerged in the water, and by the time hounds are whipped off it may well be too late. Bitches have even been known to whelp while being hunted.

Followers of otter hounds are quite prepared to wade waist-deep into rivers and waterways to baulk the quarry, but some areas of mill-pools, hatches, weirs and river cliffs are only accessible to swimming hounds. These dogs are immensely strong and powerful. The true otter hound is larger than the foxhound, and with his rough coat and grizzled muzzle may appear to the layman to be more akin to an aire-dale. They can easily out-tire an otter, particularly one in whelp, while even a dog-otter in his prime can be borne down by sheer weight of numbers.

Some of the best propaganda against otter hunting can be found in the official organ of the Buckinghamshire and Courtenay Tracy Hunt. The annual for 1966 refers to 'not an enterprising otter...caught him after forty-five minutes'. In other words, he was a spoil-sport and let himself be killed too quickly! This disposes of any claim that the hunts set out to kill pests as expeditiously as possible. This same edition refers to 'what seemed a very short five and a half hours'. To the human participants, no doubt it seemed short enough, but what about the quarry?

Time is indeed relative and one of the longest days we ever spent was out with the Buckinghamshire and Courtenay Tracy Hunt in Dorset.

The thing that struck us most at first was the general noise and sense of violence and commotion. Only a few weeks before we had walked this river, and the peace and quiet had been remarkable. There had been plenty of moorhens, ducks and herons about, and we had seen many swans and a water-vole. But now the wet heavy hounds were floundering about, flattening the vegetation on the river bank and scaring the wild life over a large area. All was noise, commotion, and uproar; humans shouting, horns trilling, hounds baying. Only the otter was silent—silently swimming for life.

A little later, the quarry appeared to have entered some fairly inaccessible drain. We were treated to a long story by one of the hunt servants about how they had drowned an otter in that very spot several years ago when the water had been higher. They could not get at him and he could not get out, but they could see his head every time he emerged for air. It is not generally known that otters cannot swim under water any longer than the rest of us, and must in fact come up for air or drown. This one drowned.

In this case the water was lower and the otter must have found some exit from his refuge; at all events, hounds were baffled. One of the masters had an engagement that evening and the hunt was called off at about 6 p.m.

After this incident we visited some of the landowners who had riparian rights on the river. In most cases we were met with a shrug. While not joining in the otter hunting, no one was going to be un-friendly enough to forbid them. No one wished to be responsible for the dearth of otters, yet no one would take the initiative to save them.

Of the twenty-two riparian owners on one stretch of the river only one really stood to lose by the presence of otters. This was a Fresh-water Biological Station where there are experimental channels (some ex-mill streams) stocked with small fry. If the otter were an enemy of anyone, it would be of such an institution. But it is significant that the Biological Station does not encourage the hunt and is in fact pro-otter.

It is equally significant that the much criticized Scott Henderson Report on Cruelty to Wild Animals, referred to the otter in the kindest terms and even described him 'playing in the water at boister-ous games with pebbles and fir-cones'. This Home Office Committee admitted that 'hunting does undoubtedly involve suffering for the otter, and the degree of it is rather greater than in most other field sports'.

Garth Christian, the eminent naturalist and a man deeply concerned for the health and economy of the countryside, wrote of the otter:

In 1949 the 13 Hunts averaging two days a week in the field between April and October, found three hundred and eighty-six otters and killed half of them. In 1953 they killed just over four hundred. In 1960 only four hundred and seventeen otters were found of which two hundred and forty were killed. A year later came ominous signs of a decline, but even so one hundred and ninety-two were killed by the hunts.

No creature is more eager than the eel to devour the eggs of the trout and the spawn and fry of other fish, and nothing copes with eels more efficiently than the otter. He will also destroy the cannibal carp and aggressive pike that disturbs the heart of the anglers. Research in Sweden and on Lake Windermere has demonstrated that on many waters the potential fish population is immense—out of all proportion to the limited food supplies. The thinning of their ranks by predators results in larger and better fed fish. Otters tend to catch the prey most easily outwitted, and so weed out the sick and the aged. Since they have a distaste for very fast flowing water, often associated with salmon it can be argued that coarse fish and eels from the quieter streams figure more often in their diet. It is significant that since otters were protected in the Towy Fishery District the annual number of Salmon caught by rods has risen from one hundred and fifty two in 1930 to one thousand three hundred and five in 1962. The Ministry of Agriculture at the time when the Otter Report of 1955 was being prepared by the Universities Federation for Animal Welfare acknowledged that compared with death from other causes, loss of fish inflicted by otters in England and Wales were quite unimportant.

Fishery officials and river boards on the whole are prepared to stand up for the otter, listing the benefits in the form of a strong population of healthy fish resulting from the otter's presence and its attention to other fish predators and diseased specimens. If there is so much good-will towards the otter, why does hunting continue?

The answer may well be that it is easier to leave a sport backed by years of tradition than to abolish it. While there are any otters remaining, we may shrug our shoulders and hope that their numbers recover and the species survives. And while we are shrugging and the hunting continues, several days a week throughout its long season, we may be nearing the point of no return, total extinction.

The badger, the oldest of our mammals, was a native Briton before the Romans arrived, and existed then as now (since myxomatosis) without his diet of rabbit, which only came into Britain with the Norman conquest. The British badger, though bear-like in appearance, is related to the stoat and weasel family. *Meles meles* is found also throughout Europe and Asia with slight variations of size and colour. He can weigh up to fifty pounds and live to be twelve years old or more.

86

Many prejudiced countrymen still believe the badger is a murderer for whom no fate is bad enough. But it is encouraging to note that those with true knowledge of the badger and his habits, through detailed and personal observation, give him an excellent character.

Soon after the war, when increased food production was imperative and agricultural pests were being considered scientifically and receiving scant mercy in the interests of higher productivity, a series on *Wild Animals and the Land* was published by the Ministry of Agriculture and Fisheries. In this publication F. Howard Lancum, the Ministry's press officer, investigated 109 cases of alleged badger damage in Devon, only one of which could be proved. In some cases the countrymen concerned with giving the badger a bad name could not differentiate between the tracks of fox and badger.

Later, Dr E. G. Neal produced a monograph on the badger after many years of studying badgers in the Cotswolds, Surrey, and Somerset. He checked the contents of many badgers' stomachs, mostly killed on the roads at night. Dr Neal's analysis discovered grass, earthworms, larvae, slugs, grubs, roots, ashfruit, unidentified seeds, acorns, beech nuts, rabbit fur and bones, dog's mercury, and water voles. No traces of poultry or lamb were found *in any of them*. These findings were in accord with F. Howard Lancum's conclusion in his *Wild Animals and the Land*, that the badger might be classed not only as no pest, but as positively the farmer's friend.

The findings of such experts (with no particular axe to grind) has had little or no effect on the countryman's attitude generally towards the badger, which is one of suspicion and hostility, although a few enlightened farmers of the younger generation may leave any badgers on their land in peace. The rest are always willing to 'have a go' at him.

In this connection it is interesting to note Dr Neal's comment: 'This is in no way a book on sport, but brief reference must be made to badger digging and baiting...When I was first asked if I would like to go to a badger digging I was asked if I were squeamish, because, it was said, "the end is not always very pleasant"'.

When one of the participants can warn a scientific observer of 'unpleasantness' we have found it can safely be taken that this is an understatement. Dr Neal continues:

> If an animal causes harm then there is a logical reason for destroying it; but when it is *well-proved* that the good it does far outweighs the occasional harm, why do we go on persecuting it? Truly we are an illogical race.

This is another understatement. Perhaps we are a bloodthirsty race needing the merest excuse to kill. Sometimes we do not need any excuse at all, the fact that another creature dares to live and share our countryside with us being enough to make us persecute it to the death. There is little that science or education or enlightened reasoning can do against the closed mind. To many dyed-in-the-wool countrymen (and we write as lifelong country-dwellers), the badger is a wild beast to be killed. He is a *bad* thing, a nocturnal animal to be feared because not much is known about him. We fear the unknown, and fear breeds cruelty. Neal puts it like this:

> Ignorance about the badger is appalling. Few people have ever seen one alive although they may live in an area where they are common. They inconsequentially assume that they *do* harm, and when the chance comes they destroy the badger. The majority of farmers and gamekeepers behave in this way, and when the word goes round that there are badgers in such and such a place, there is soon a willing gang ready to dig them out and kill them.

We have found this all too true in Devon, Somerset, and Dorset, and from RSPCA reports it would appear to be true of most other counties as well. One man near Bath boasted in the columns of the well-known farming journal, *Farmer's Weekly* (23 November 1962), that he and his 'brave terriers' had killed over sixty badgers in one season.

Henry Williamson, the writer and naturalist, described such a badger dig in his *Tales of a Devon Village*. Used as he was to the rough pastimes of a hard-living community, he commented on the unnecessary brutality and the amount of beer required to keep up the courage of the sportsmen, and observed that liquor was never drunk in a less worthy cause.

Badger-digging is still a favourite pursuit in many parts of the West Country. Briefly, this is the procedure. A terrier is sent down into the sett (as a badger's earth is called) to engage the quarry, who otherwise might dig himself out at the other end. If the terrier is tired or badly bitten or retreats, having had enough, reinforcements can be sent in, as each terrier-owner is anxious for his dog to prove his worth and courage. Indeed one of the defences of badger digging which have been repeatedly put to us by those engaged in it is that it improves the breed of terrier. How any dog is improved by being badly bitten and mauled by the steely-strong jaws of a badger is difficult to understand. When Lee stated in his *Natural History* that the badger was hard to kill, he was right, and this is what *makes* the sport of badger digging. The badger does not run away, or give up, or submit; he usually fights to his last breath, terribly mauled, heavily outnumbered by dogs tearing his flesh, humans aiming blows at him; broken, battered, bleeding, he will fight literally to the death.

While the terriers are engaging him, the human participants dig their way in with frequent pauses for refreshment. There is usually no lack of willing helpers and the work can proceed in relays. The only digging machine which the badger possesses are his claws. By the end of a dig, these may be worn down to the pad.

At the end, if the badger is required alive for further sport (i.e. baiting), or if it is thought that the terriers have received enough punishment, or if the diggers want to be in a better position to deliver the long-delayed *coup de grâce*, badger-tongs are employed to drag the animal the last few feet into the open.

We find that relatively few countrymen have ever seen these tongs outside an agricultural bygones museum, but they are still in use and are still being manufactured. Nowadays they may be hastily 'knocked up' by a local smith or even by one of the diggers themselves. These implements, which exert tremendous pressure, may be left with rough jagged edges which further inflict quite horrible wounds through the interlocking action of their pincer-like ends. The tongs are usually about four feet long, heavy, and cumbersome to use accurately (i.e. to 'collar' the badger).

Ruth Murray of Point Nature Reserve in Devon has made a special study of badgers, after rescuing them whenever possible and bringing them up with her more domestic animals. In this way she has learned at first hand their qualities and possibilities, and her findings, published in articles and in book form, reinforce that persecution is unwarranted.

In the sixties, Frederick Burden, MP for Gillingham and chairman of the all-party Animal Welfare Committee, tried to bring a bill to make badger-digging illegal. It was revealed that while many farmers dig to serve the 'interests of agriculture', countrymen in remoter parts of Britain still go badger-digging for sport. When the bill was proposed, enterprising journalists went in search of evidence from the badger-diggers themselves.

One man from Okehampton in Devon declared that he 'liked to see dogs pitting their wits against the badger'. Obviously in a bygone age he would have been a candidate for a seat at the Colosseum. The bill was not successful, and badger-digging is still not illegal, though many animal welfare societies have worked to make it so. Ruth Murray, with her wide experience of the barbarities of this particular sport, has collected enough evidence to sink a royal commission and has made direct representation to the Home Office. But while the case is still being pleaded, the badger is still being persecuted under the most brutal circumstances.

If digging as a means of extermination is still lawful, badger-*baiting* technically is not. With cock-fighting and similar kinds of country entertainment (often with betting involved), it is illegal. And like cock-fighting, it is just as hard to stamp out, particularly in the wilder parts of Britain, where it has gone underground. The RSPCA and, to a lesser degree perhaps, the police, get wind of baiting from time to time. Reports have come from Carmarthen, from the hills and fells of Cumberland, and from the wilder parts of Somerset and Devon. Discovery and conviction are notoriously difficult. Getting wind of, then tracking down and uncovering, a bait is impossible without inside information and then may involve trespass and possibly physical danger (though badger-diggers themselves frequently trespass).

The participants are too well known to each other for an outsider to pass unnoticed. A badger dug out as a pest on private land can be transported to some barn or out-building without let or hindrance. The sport is to pit the badger against a series of dogs to see who owns the best animal. The sport will continue until the badger has had enough, which virtually means when he is dead, and he may take quite a long time to die.

In places where digging is impracticable and baiting too dangerous to be practised, badgers may be gassed, snared or trapped. The gin-trap has been illegal in Britain since the Act banning its use was passed in 1958, but this is generally taken to apply to the rabbit gin. Larger traps for foxes and badgers can still be obtained, and are on sale from agricultural merchants in some cases, although an undertaking must be signed that these are not to be used for rabbits and a note in small print declares that they may only be sold outside England and Wales.

It is interesting to note that this Act, which humane-minded people had pressed for long before the last war, only came into force when myxomatosis had rendered it virtually unnecessary and had in any case put the rabbit-trapper out of work.

Fox and badger traps are larger and heavier than the common rabbit gin and are capable of inflicting dreadful damage on any animal caught in them. Similarly, a snare acts through slow or part strangulation, and it is not difficult to snare a badger as he is very much a creature of habit and will use the same route (making a well-worn path) from his sett night after night. The snare holds the badger, biting the wire and struggling until inspected many hours, even days later, when it may be killed, usually brutally. Often the carcase is found, only long after the snare was set.

Remote farms with rough woodland, wild heathy areas, copses far removed from any public road, afford perfect protection for anyone engaged in killing badgers. If to know of these barbarities is to interfere, how can one interfere without incurring the penalties of trespass? Beware, too, of coming between the countryman and his pleasures — even those in authority have jibbed at doing just that.

During the last few years, badger feasts have become popular. Certain West Country public houses have found this kind of occasion very good for business and even go as far as to serve these feasts in seventeenth-century costume. Many people out of curiosity want to taste badger 'hams' and here is a legitimate excuse for the diggers and baiters and the 'ridding-the-farms-of-pests' sportsmen not only to indulge in their sport but to make money out of it. A change from Thanksgiving suppers or roasting oxen in the market place is a badger feast. Widely advertised, they have caught on. When asked how the badgers were killed, you will be solemnly told that they were shot.

The RSPCA is called in by indignant critics of the feast only when the badger is dead meat and it is difficult to prove anything. Although humane people have been outraged by this new reason for killing badgers, the defendants can quite rightly suggest that if the end-product can be eaten no one can now suggest killing is simply for fun.

There are other end-products to the badger besides his meat, now described as a cross between pork and venison. For centuries badger bristle has been used in shaving brushes, and it seems that no other animal has hair quite so suitable for this purpose, although shaving brushes can now be made of synthetic fibres. Badger grease was a sovereign remedy for all kinds of ailments, and since tradition dies hard with older country people, a small pot of badger grease may still fetch as much as thirty shillings. It is reputed to cure baldness and infertility (among other things), and indeed Mrs Murray in her investigations into badger-digging and baiting in Devon and Cornwall has come to the conclusion that there is more involved in this badger persecution than just sport. This nocturnal and secretive animal, denied the publicity afforded the fox by his status in hunting circles, has a certain aura of ancient magic surrounding him, even in this twentieth century. People believe what they want to believe. The badger is an unusual animal, bear-like and uncommon, nocturnal and hard to kill, inordinately fond of honey. It might explain his purpose in the rural scheme of things to believe that he is connected with fertility.

It is said that he eats eggs (ask any gamekeeper) and will rob the beehive as well as the wasps' nest. Eggs and honey are well-known aphrodisiacs; might not the flesh and grease of the badger be even more powerful?

In 1967 many people were shocked at news of the wanton slaughter of a family of badgers, which included cubs, at a school at St Gorran, near Helston, in Cornwall.

The young pupils had taken a great and proprietory interest in their badger family, watching them, noting their habits and being passionately interested in their welfare. One morning the badger sett was found to have been raided, and the inmates had gone, amid every sign of violence and mayhem. The wanton nature of this destruction, which also involved trespass (as is so often the case with badger killers), and the distress of the children who were being educated to think humanely about our wild life, resulted in a great deal of publicity. The children's distress, perhaps more than the suffering to badgers which was involved in this incident, was the cause of headline news and much strong feeling. Ruth Murray was one of the people called in by the school to take up the children's case and to investigate the killing. Why were these badgers slaughtered? For spite? For their 'magical' properties? For the sake of their pelts, which can sell for a pound or more and which are much prized by scooterists and motor-bike enthusiasts as trophies?

In Dorset, the army firing ranges between Lulworth and Kimmeridge include the ruined village of Tyneham, where there has been a large badger colony for centuries. Over the Easter holiday in 1968 when the range was open to the public, we visited the sett, found the holes blocked, terrier paw prints and boot marks all about, heavy cudgels thrown down and every evidence of another 'Gorran'. These badgers were not near livestock or poultry, for generations they have braved the guided missile rockets and the heavy reverberations of gunfire. And now they have been dug out and destroyed. The badger may have occupied one sett continuously for hundreds of years, as was the case with the army range sett. He is clean; there are no mangy badgers. In particular, his latrines are well away from the sett, and he even spring-cleans his underground home and regularly turns out the 'bedding'. Meanwhile, all too often the countryman who lives alongside the badger is adamant that he is an evil creature. He moves at night, he smells, and above all he has the temerity to face up to man and defend himself—to the often bitter end.

# 7

## *The Food We Eat*

'A man is what he eats.'
LUDWIG FEUERBACH (1804–1872)

Animal husbandry in the twentieth century has become a subject that does not lie easily upon the public conscience. Many people in this civilized western hemisphere are by no means happy about the conditions under which our food is produced. One of their worst fears was confirmed when Ruth Harrison published her report on modern methods of livestock rearing in her book, *Animal Machines*. The term 'factory farming' was always good for a news headline, and in Britain the subject has been kept before the public while the Brambell Committee debated the subject and published its findings and recommendations.

Ultra-modern methods of keeping livestock, while open to abuse, are not the only cause of disquiet on the farming front; there are others which are taken too much for granted.

Most agricultural communities, particularly in the more remote areas, have at least one holding in their midst which is sub-standard. It may be too small to be a financial success and the owner may work elsewhere part-time, often as a scrap or general dealer or as odd-job man or drover at markets and auctions. His holding may be very badly run and his livestock neglected. He manages to stay on the right side of the law and the humane societies and just clear of the courts as somehow he muddles through. Some landlords turn a blind eye to such tenants, either because they are members of old families who have farmed there for generations or because the tenant is an old man whose days are numbered. The local body of the National Farmers Union are only likely to step in where a holding is so badly cultivated that it constitutes a real waste of land or a danger in the matter of spreading weeds or 'agricultural pests' to neighbouring holdings. These small farmers (and sometimes not so small) scratch a living and manage to walk the razor's edge between what is legal and what is not, but it is always their livestock who suffer. It is the animal husbandry side of their farming which gives rise to most concern among humane people.

In Britain, a man can do much as he pleases with his own beasts, and the police or RSPCA inspectors cannot be in every field, copse or barn to watch what a man does with his own property. If they are called in by some specific complaint they can act, but an employee is unlikely to report cruelty or mismanagement, and quite often this type of small farmer has no employees but his own family.

Three cases of which we have first-hand experience illustrate this type of farming or small-holding only too well. The first was in a Somerset village during a severe winter. A man with a full-time job on a nearby Army camp rented a field and stocked it with six heifers. He usually visited them after work, about six o'clock in the evening, bringing them a bale or two of hay. When the nights drew in he visited them every other evening, then when ice and snow made the roads tricky, about once a week. The small pond in the field froze over. Cattle in the surrounding fields were well supplied with hay and water. A neighbouring farmer broke the ice on the pond for the six animals every morning when visiting his own beasts. Small amounts of hay were given to help them subsist, which meant that they were not actually starving. If this slight help had stopped and these heifers had actually starved, the RSPCA could have prosecuted. The neighbour could not watch them starve, so the animals led a miserable and precarious existence, in poor condition, just short of starvation, before being sent for slaughter.

The second case was of an old couple who kept a few sheep in a small orchard, as a source of income. The animals were on inadequate rations and appeared in very poor condition. These people were not deliberately cruel, they simply had insufficient means to maintain them healthily. No one could say (unlike the first case) that they neglected to tend their animals and left them to the charity of neighbours. These people lived almost *with* their animals, but that did not prevent the sheep from being half-starved and riddled with disease in their bare muddy enclosure.

The last case concerned a farmer who had the means and ample fodder but was casual in his methods and neglected to look round his out-wintering dry cows with sufficient regularity to prevent one of them seeking shelter in an outlying barn and dying in an advanced state of emaciation which the prosecuting veterinary surgeon likened to

94

a 'concentration camp victim'. In this case, the law and the RSPCA stepped in, but by that time the cow, after more than two weeks' neglect in severe weather, was past all help and was dying when the veterinary surgeon reached her. These three cases are very ordinary ones which can undoubtedly be multiplied in many different areas.

Why should such things happen when farming has been taken out of the dark ages of muck and mystery and has become mechanically sophisticated? How does such unnecessary neglect or cruelty continue in an industry that is solvent and thriving? It is largely because many people, who are quite unfitted for the job, keep animals. Ideally there should be some fitness test applied before a man has charge of livestock, rather like a driving test before he is left in sole charge of a car. But this is about as impossible as a fit-to-be-parents test applied before anyone is allowed to have children.

In the past, the unskilled man who could obtain work nowhere else would find employment on a farm or small-holding. Many of us have seen louts in charge of animals missing no opportunity of administering a blow or a kick, whether merited or not. There are enlightened and humane stockmen, but we have had personal experience of others whom we would not trust with any living creature.

Unfortunately many new-generation countrymen and their wives often prefer to do factory work which pays better and offers them more freedom, less responsibility, and a much shorter working week. Farm work is still badly paid in comparison with other industries, entails long hours, much patience and good humour, and is in fact a real vocation, but it does not always attract the men it deserves. Sometimes men who are fitted for nothing else can rent a piece of ground, buy a few animals at market, sell them at a profit, and they are in the livestock business. We may eat the result of their labours, but it is food sometimes produced under the worst possible conditions for the beast.

In Britain one of the fallacies latent in stock-farming is that we have a temperate climate. We do in fact suffer extremes of temperature in most years. Few winters pass by without a freeze-up. Cattle will withstand the cold if it is dry. Our winters are composed of periods when it is both wet and cold. Then it is not unusual to see livestock up to their bellies in freezing mud, humped up against the driving, icy rain looking thoroughly miserable. Often their pastures have no shelter beyond a few strands of barbed wire. Modern farming tends to grub out thick hedges as uneconomic. The hay and other fodder given these outwintering animals is consumed in keeping up bodily heat, rather than in contributing to flesh or milk. Yet, year after year, to save housing space or cleaning out, livestock, including milking herds, are left outside, sometimes day and night. On the Continent, when the first snows of winter are threatening, livestock are brought safely under cover, and fed on the spot with little wastage.

In periods of freezing rainfall when the telegraph wires have been sheathed in ice we have seen miserable sheep, half frozen to the ground, cattle, pigs and ponies dispiritedly standing, backs to the icy storms, with nowhere to go out of the wind, no lee of hillside or cover as they would have in the wild state, and with no dry place to lie down.

Lambs are born out of doors in the bitterest of weather, often with the merest hurdle to shelter them from freezing winds. Some farming friends who have a large area of exposed high land tried for the first time last year to turn a large barn into lambing pens, divided with hay bales. It created a good deal of extra work, but they were repaid a hundredfold by trouble-free births and no orphan lambs. Continental farmers cannot understand why we have not made a habit of this long ago.

And so we come to the other end of the scale, to the man who, to cut labour costs, brings his entire stock indoors *for the whole of their lives*. This has become known as intensive farming. Some of the larger so-called 'factory' farmers are not husbandmen in the old sense at all, but businessmen attempting to produce a conveyor-belt food-product of uniform size, weight and quality. Hence we get broiler chicken, battery eggs, baby beef, 'sweatbox' pigs, and battery veal.

Free-range poultry may lay their eggs over a wide area, waste much of the grain thrown to them, and have to be penned in safely at night. In addition, their eggs may get broken, stolen, and in bad weather be extremely dirty. But just one man can look after ten thousand hens in a battery house which is fully automatic and the figure for the future is put at twenty thousand. Food is measured, each bird getting just the correct ration, the eggs are clean, uniform and unbroken. There is some wastage among the birds, which have become virtually egg-laying machines, but the production numbers are so enormous and the turn-over so vast that a certain percentage of birds are expendable. In order to turn hens into more efficient laying machines, wings are cut to save space in the battery system cages, beaks are trimmed to avoid feather pecking and cannibalism (brought on by boredom and immobility), and combs are cut to induce an early moult in laying-birds and hasten egg production.

Similar conditions apply to pigs in Danish-type units. One man can feed, water and clean out hundreds of pigs, which in old-type houses with outside runs would be impossible. The pigs convert their food into pork or bacon at an economic ratio. This food conversion can be controlled, and the pig graded at just the desired weight and state of fatness or leanness required by the market. It knows no change of atmosphere and at birth is liable to iron deficiency which can be made up by injections; a tendency to disease from its hot-house existence is combated by modern drugs, particularly of the antibiotic range.

Defenders of factory farming point to hens scratching in the mud and say their eggs must be unhygienic and the hens themselves miserable in bad weather. There may be no denying either point, but equally a hen plainly takes a delight in scratching for at least part of its food, likes to pick and choose and have a diet in season, and most certainly free-range eggs have deeper yolks and less watery whites and are more satisfactory for cooking in many ways.

When it comes to pigs, it seems inhumane to keep them in so-called sweatbox piggeries at the recommended rate of three feet per pig and at a temperature of eighty degrees. The joy and abandon with which free-range pigs, or even those with an open sty, will root about would point to the iniquity of immobilizing them from birth to the bacon factory. American farmers do not even wait for the moment of birth, because hysterectomy is now widely practised in the United States of America. The whole uterus is removed with piglets inside it, and the offspring are kept in sterile incubators to form the basis of disease-free herds.

In direct contrast to this, a letter to the *Farmers Weekly* describes how the writer hired a derelict building for keeping pigs. The staircase was intact and the pigman reported that the animals availed themselves of the whole house, ran up and down stairs and in and out of the rooms at will. He concluded that these were the best pigs he had ever had. This tends to prove that pigs, like humans (and come to that, most other animals as well) thrive on a certain amount of variety, and dislike complete monotony and boredom.

To many of us the worst aspect of factory farming lies in some of the production methods of battery veal. Calves taken from their mothers at birth are immobilized either by tethering or by being put into crates or even occasionally with their heads in 'stocks' so that they cannot lick any part of the pen or flooring and thereby pick up any vestige of iron. The aim is to keep them anaemic and so produce the whitest possible meat. They cannot groom or lick themselves, and anyone who has ever been immobilized in a hospital bed or with limbs in plaster knows the torment of being unable to move freely. For cleaning purposes they are kept on slatted floors, which is anathema to cloven-footed animals (hence the success of cattle grids) and results in deformed feet and swollen joints. These young animals are fed with a calf gruel or milk substitute but are given no water. The gruel makes them thirsty and there is nothing to slake that thirst but another dose of gruel; consequently they grow and put on weight. These calves are given a maximum of fifteen weeks to live. After that the extreme anaemia induced by their mode of living and diet would cause death in any case, if they were not slaughtered first. Antibiotics as an aid to growth and a deterrent to a too-early death are freely employed. No one can pretend this is exactly rude health, but the words 'happy' or 'content' and 'thriving' are repeatedly employed by veal producers.

We once inspected a battery house for the production of veal, accompanied by an RSPCA Senior Inspector. The animals were in almost complete darkness, which was broken only when their shutters were raised at feeding time. The house had an indescribable sickly-sweet smell. It was not the smell of honest muck and healthy livestock, but a smell of sickness and decay. The Inspector's wife said that this sickly stench clung to her husband's uniform for days afterwards.

The moment one criticizes this method of farming the producers reply with some heat that these intensive methods greatly increase production and that there is a 'world food shortage'.

John Cherrington, who farms on a large scale in Hampshire and who has written and broadcast extensively on farming topics, has declared:

> I have never agreed with the common view that there is a danger of world food shortage. There may be *world hunger*, in that some countries and some people haven't the means of producing or buying their food. But there is no commercial shortage...All I can say from experience and information is that there is more undeveloped, unused land of good cropping potential in the world than is being farmed today. *Surpluses* are with us for a very long time to come.

Because of this imbalance we can still hear of wheat being burnt, of fruit rotting, of fish catches thrown back into the sea, because the price was not right; of crops standing unwanted in silos, of vegetables that cannot be given away, of coffee 'dumped' and bananas going bad. We are pressed to drink more milk, to eat more eggs, because of over-production. We import eggs cheaply and our own egg producers have to find more and more short cuts to making a profit of any kind. Men who invested capital in enormous battery houses have been known to go broke and leave rotting buildings and piles of stinking guano together with the swarms of flies and colonies of rodents that accompany such ventures, as their sole memorial in a farming countryside.

Battery veal will not help to feed anyone starving in India or Mexico or Africa. In Britain it is a luxury food for the affluent society, and the greatest customers of the whitemeat industry are hotels and restaurants. It is hypocrisy to stress that there is a world food shortage and in the same breath slaughter cattle at *only* fifteen weeks old.

Many farmers jumped on the egg-producer's bandwagon only to find it let them down. Many of these same farmers who live within easy reach of large centres of population have found it pays to advertise free-range eggs and sell at the door.

The *Farmer and Stockbreeder* journal recognized this fact in an editorial recently when it suggested that one way in which farmers could beat an adverse price review was by dealing in 'quality products' direct to the mobile customer—fresh cream, free-range, large, brown eggs, home-grown vegetables including potatoes, oven-ready chickens and poultry (not battery hens or broiler chicks), and home-made jams and country preserves.

In a letter to the *Illustrated London News* on 20 January 1968, J. Bower of the Farm and Food Society stated:

> It is undeniable that salmonella (poisoning) has become much more widespread due to factory farming—For example Mr H. I. Field, Director of Veterinary Laboratories and the Veterinary Inspection Service of the Ministry of Agriculture writes that 'The increased importance of salmonellosis in calves is another example of a disease which has become of major concern under intensive systems of calf-rearing. Salmonellosis in cattle is nothing new—but it remained economically unimportant until systems of husbandry were introduced which were favourable to the organisms concerned.
>
> Anti-biotics are used liberally in an attempt to minimise the losses. They are even used as a universal panacea in an attempt to combat the "dysadaptation syndrome" that results when calves are so badly treated. Yet in some units as many as ten per cent to fifteen per cent affected, die of this dysadaptation syndrome. And the number of calves dying of salmonella infection has increased about ten times during the last eight years.

As long ago as November 1960 the late John Dugdale, MP, presented a bill to the House of Commons to 'secure humane conditions and practices in connection with the rearing and keeping in buildings of animals for the production of food.' *Hansard* records that the bill was to be read a second time on 24 March 1961. No second reading took place.

The views of the then Minister of Agriculture (Mr Christopher

Soames) were made clear in reply to a question from Dr King, who subsequently became Speaker of the House of Commons. Dr King asked the Minister if he would institute an enquiry into the intensive methods of food production now being used to provide white veal and chickens by the broiler and battery systems, with a view to ending unnecessary cruelty.

The Minister replied that an enquiry was not necessary; there was already the 1911 Act which covered all animals including calves and chickens.

But of course in 1911 modern techniques and methods, from conveyor-belt feeding to wonder drugs, had not been heard of and could hardly have been visualized. It is interesting to note that a power failure overnight or at a weekend when an employee was off duty has more than once resulted in the death of hundreds of hens. Dr King asked:

> Is the Minister aware that most people, including most farmers, would agree that the creatures we kill for food have a right to live naturally before we take their lives? Would he not agree that under new intensive methods of food production there is unnaturalness and unnecessary cruelty?

Mr Soames replied:

> The Hon. Member referred to living naturally but the whole process of domestication of animals can be regarded as interference with nature. There is a difference of opinion about the degree of interference, but the experiments which have been carried out on this type of rearing of animals show that it certainly can be done without cruelty. What we should bear in mind is that if this is to be a successful operation the animal must thrive, and that if there is a question of cruelty and the animal is suffering it does not thrive—and there is no evidence to show that.

John Cherrington, writing as a farmer in the *Financial Times* of 6 November 1964, answered the Minister's argument in retrospect:

> Those who defend these methods point out that the animals eat well, and either lay well or put on weight, and this is an indication of the lack of cruelty. Unhappy animals it is argued would not thrive. I don't think this is a conclusive argument at all. Confined as they are, they have nothing else to do but eat, and the ingredients in their scientifically blended feeds make their bodies do the rest.

In the spring of 1964 Ruth Harrison's *Animal Machines* appeared. The reviewers took it up, devoted the kind of space and attention to it that they had lavished on its American forerunner, *Silent Spring*, by Rachel

Carson. That book dealt largely with the use of pesticides and weed-killers on insect and therefore bird population and the ultimate effect on our lives. Miss Harrison, concerned with the food we eat and its effect upon us, also laid great emphasis, as the title implies, on the use and abuse of live creatures in this new type of farming.

The mixers and compounders of scientifically balanced feeding stuffs had been having a field-day. The manufacturers of battery equipment, mechanized feeding and cleaning appliances were doing wonderful business. Miss Harrison was not only up against the farming industry which believed it had found the panacea for all its financial ills and labour troubles; she was up against that old enemy of humane reform, vested interest.

But the press caught hold of her book and the correspondence columns of even the farming journals would not let it go.

When *Animal Machines* was published the Ministry of Agriculture had a press conference at which they put up ten of their experts to answer questions on the book. Their Chief Scientific Adviser, Sir Harold Sanders, made the comment, 'no case has been established for making it an offence merely to deprive animals of light, freedom to exercise or pasture'. The word 'merely' irritated a great many people.

Animals without daylight, exercise or fresh food, beasts kept alive by drugs, immobilized to put on weight more quickly, not being allowed to dissipate one ounce of their intake by even the exercise of scratching themselves, kept on concrete in their own filth, or on slats to save cleaning out, staggering to the slaughter house on deformed limbs, or, in the case of poultry, being thrown alive into boiling 'plucking' vats. Could this be true? Could this be right?

Pictures were published, vets weighed in with evidence—not all of them on the side of their clients, the intensive farmers.

The *Daily Telegraph* in an article referred to 'oestrogens and auro-mycin during growth, tranquillisers during the journey to slaughter, and intravenous injections just before death to make cold storage unnecessary and result in tender meat'.

On 24 May, in *The Guardian*, Dame Margery Perham asked:

> Are animal factories *progress*, or are they another move in the advance of the machine which is dividing man from man, and now man from animal?—For myself, I believe man lowers his own civilisation by treating the animal world, which has been put wholly into his power, as if living creatures were *things*.—are we to see nothing but rows of giant factory buildings packed to the last square inch in their dark interiors with almost motionless creatures?

The *Economist* declared there is no mystery about the economics of the 'concrete farm'.

> It is mass production and automation applied to animal rearing. Suppose a beast can be induced to put on weight faster than nature intended; it is likely to fetch a lower price at market, but as the farm will sell more beasts over a given period, the net profit could be higher. This is the old, old story of smaller margins and a higher turnover; in this case there happens also to be an inevitable reduction in quality simply because young animals have less flavour than developed ones.— The animals do best in the sense of most rapidly converting feed into saleable meat, if they are confined in the smallest possible space—the farm becomes an assembly line within which the beasts spend their lives, where they can be stocked at many times the density possible in an open field and where feeding and cleaning are handled mechanically, with the minimum of labour—the factory farmer does not depend on fields.

Edward Hyams in the *New Statesman* took an even more positive view:

> We do not know that the stuff injected into these animals will have no effect on ourselves...the method of production is without a shadow of doubt, continuously and abominably cruel...

In 1964 the RSPCA wrote to the Minister of Agriculture drawing attention to reports published in the *Observer* and other newspapers concerning Ruth Harrison's book and asking for the setting up of a departmental committee to enquire into the whole problem of intensive farming.

The Minister replied that he was not satisfied that an enquiry was needed. The controversy continued. At the end of April 1964, when questioned by Mr F. F. A. Burden (an MP noted for his interest in humane treatment of animals), the Minister announced the decision to set up a committee.

The chairman appointed was Professor F. W. Rogers Brambell and the terms of reference were set out by the Minister on 29 June 1964. Three 'officials' were on the Brambell Committee and six 'eminent outsiders'. These last included a veterinary surgeon and Lady Barnett.

The findings of the Brambell Committee were published in 1966. Their recommendations fell far short of the improved conditions some had hoped for, but they did lay down a definite minimum standard of living for our animals. For instance, they recommended that all live-stock, from barley beef to battery hens, should have room to turn round, stand up or lie down, and groom themselves.

This seems a very minimal concession. For instance, five hens in one battery cage (which is not unusual) are packed so closely they can perform none of these essential natural actions.

Ruth Harrison, having formed an advisory group of seven to convey evidence to the Brambell Committee, with two eminent veterinary surgeons among her experts, had worked towards more humane concessions. Her recommendations covered transport of livestock, practices such as de-beaking of fowls, types of building, use of antibiotics, and standards of slaughterhouses and slaughter methods.

The Brambell Report boiled down to the minimum of help for animals and the maximum that the farming community would take in the way of 'interference'. It was little enough to ask. Many food reform enthusiasts felt it was quite inadequate; the rest of us perhaps decided it was better than nothing. It was a start.

But even this minimum of help for the helpless was delayed. The Ministry of Agriculture, backed by pressure from the National Farmers Union, made no prompt move to implement the findings of the Brambell Committee which had already been a couple of years in reaching the light of day. Newspapers took up the delay, correspondence was aired (more briefly this time) and the topic sank from the headlines again. A farmer born and bred who had handled livestock for almost half a century ironically quoted the playwright Simon Raven's words, 'A Court of Enquiry must find out all the facts in order that they may be successfully suppressed'.

We had seen this happen over the training methods for circus animals and over the Henderson Committee report on Wild Animals, after the failure of the 1948 bill to ban the hunting of deer, otter and hares for sport. The general public are lulled by these reports into thinking that the matter has been fully investigated by those best fitted to do so, the subject is in good hands, and so the rest of us can safely leave it to 'them'.

Mr Frank Paton, one-time Member of Parliament and one of the biggest battery-veal producers in Britain, made devaluation a handy weapon to use against the reformists. In a letter to the *Farmer and Stockbreeder* in December 1967 he wrote:

> If this government are serious about their intentions for agriculture to play its part in the national recovery, then any suggestion of legislation which will hamper progress in the developments of livestock production methods must be forgotten forthwith. What is certain is that there is no MP qualified to speak on intensive systems, never mind vote on a new law, and I have yet to meet a single experienced Ministry Officer or scientist in this country or in Europe who would be dogmatic on any standards whatsoever. If the Government are sincere about agricul-

ture's future they should remove the severe lack of confidence which
Brambell has caused without further ado and unequivocally.

Mr Paton had a deep vested interest in retaining his battery-veal-
producing methods, and in the form of a great deal of capital tied up in
his factory farming equipment, but to declare that no MP was capable
of assessing inhumane treatment of farm animals is patently untrue.
John Dugdale and F. F. A. Burden were both MPs with experience of
farming, who had tried to inaugurate some reforms. Many sympathetic
MPs had first-hand knowledge of farming conditions or had humane-
minded farmers willing to give evidence on animal husbandry, among
their constituents.

We are greatly indebted to the dairy cow for milk, one of the staple
ingredients of western civilization's health-giving body-building
diets, which together with her by-products of cream, cheese and butter
and canned and dried milk-products represent health and wealth to
millions. Our bottlefed babies and thriving schoolchildren represent
the health side of it, our huge dairy industry and the ice cream and
milk-producing industries represent the wealth. Yet we turn the cow
into a continuously pregnant animal, often with hormone-induced
births resulting in damage. Then we take away the calf or calves almost
at birth in order to use the milk ourselves. She probably was not mated
with a bull but served by artificial insemination and is deprived of
being naturally mated when on heat and suckling her offspring after
she has given birth. In the words of one vet, she is now neither mate
nor mother. We then dehorn her, dock her tail so that she cannot even
remove flies from her flanks. When old and worn out from being used
like a milking machine, we send her off to the slaughterhouse, which
may involve long rail and sea journeys.

Meanwhile, in our headlong progress towards producing more and
more from less and less, our farm birds and beasts are turned into
conversion units—from grain to meat, or grass to milk, or gruel to
veal, while Nature is eliminated as far as possible.

In September 1968 the Ministry of Agriculture published a report
*Calf Wastage and Husbandry in Britain 1962–3*, which gives details of
calf losses that are surprising in the second half of our twentieth
century. The survey covered records of about 40,000 calves reared on
more than 1,500 farms. 5.44 per cent were aborted or still-born. 4.98
per cent died or were *sold for slaughter or rearing before their first feed.*
Out of 3,400,000 born alive and given their first feed, 89,000 died
within a month of birth, and 19,000 brought-in animals, within a month
of purchase.

About the same time, the University Federation for Animal Welfare stated that 'chickens hatch and die on rubbish dumps': discarded day-old male chicks were 'chucked into polythene bags and suffocated under their own weight'.

Major Scott, speaking at an annual meeting of the Federation, said some sixty to eighty million male chicks were disposed of yearly, some of them being tipped into bins and splashed with irritating liquid chloroform or tetrachloride. 'The responsibility of the poultry industry to adopt reasonable standards of animal welfare is quite clear. Its financial ability to carry these out is beyond dispute.' Meanwhile, the Brambell Report findings, much watered-down, were presented to the general public and farming community as a Draft Code for the welfare of farm animals. The code is less kind to animals than the original Brambell Report. It lays down one square foot of space for seven pounds per liveweight broiler. In rearing cages the normal density should not exceed eight pounds liveweight per square foot of floor area. For adult battery birds the suggested maximum density is ten pounds a square foot where three or more birds are housed together.

A good exercise here is to mark out a square foot of floor space and then pile ten one-pound bags or packets of sugar on to it. A hen with lesser density, counting areas such as wing and neck and room occupied by feet and feathers, will occupy more space than the sugar, but she must spend her entire life in her cage with that amount of room. The code states that debeaking may be necessary, but hopes that future developments may render dewinging, pinioning and notching or tendon severing where it involves mutilation of wing tissue unnecessary.

Sir Thomas Bazely, writing in the *Daily Telegraph* on 9 September 1968, questioning the defenders of factory farming in poultry, asks:

> If the health of broilers is so perfect, why did the taxpayer have to pay compensation in respect of fowl pest (slaughter of birds) to the amount of over three million pounds in 1960–61 and more than double the following year? Broilers also suffer extensively from cancer, chronic respiratory disease and leucosis, but they may not *die* of the disease since they are killed when nine or ten weeks old.
> Battery hens have cancer in eight different organs; also diseases of the liver, digestion and kidneys ('pullets' disease') among others. Some diseases are suppressed by means of antibiotics but this is 'a substitute for good husbandry'. (*Farmer and Stockbreeder*, 1 May 1962).

Under the new code (approved in October 1969 by the House of Commons) it is also suggested that the new-born calf should receive colostrum from its dam for the first six hours of its life, if it is not be be *slaughtered at once*. Just how, on thousands of farms, all these suggested codes of practice are to be implemented it is difficult to see. Calves have no set hours to be born, and the mind boggles at the thought of an inspector standing by in the small hours of the night on some remote farm to make certain that the newly born calf is allowed to suckle its dam. We are back to square one: it is the farmer or the farm worker who in the end is the arbiter of an animal's fate, and legislation can be only the springboard to advancement. Education, public opinion, a change of heart or of outlook about the animals we eat are the only sure, if very slow, way to improvement.

And all the time new ways are being discovered and perfected to make our food animals produce more meat for less keep.

However, the British Veterinary Association and the Royal College of Veterinary Surgeons submitted evidence to a committee considering the possible dangers of 'feed additives' for growth promotion. The BVA strongly recommended that 'wherever possible, use of anti-bacterial agents should be confined to drugs not commonly used in the treatment of disease in animals or man.' They commented on the commercial pressures to buy and use such agents and stated that most farmers still opt for the bottle and syringe when in trouble. In experiments at Weybridge veterinary laboratory, pigs became clinically ill after six days on the level of 2,000 grams of additives per ton. The first sign of trouble was a slow tremor of the head with staring eyes, progressive inability to coordinate the limbs and increasing blindness.

The demand for cheap food, the cut-throat competition not only between farms and markets but between countries and exporting interests, results in a constant chase after cost-cutting. Everything from cheese to beef is hurried along. Quantity is all, quality is secondary. More chicken, beef or whatever, at a lower cost; and if the flavour does not measure up to the old more gently matured product, the modern housewife and the family budget are still satisfied. So new ways are being thought up to produce more meat in a shorter time. Force feeding or 'cramming' is not confined to Strasbourg geese and the production of *pâté de foie gras*. It is recommended for table poultry, particularly capons, in Britain. Here is a description of the method from *Modern Poultry Husbandry* of 1961.

> The cramming machine stands on a tripod. It consists of a food container fitted with a plunger operated by a pedal. When the latter is pressed food is forced through a rubber tube which the crammer inserts in the bird's throat, the end of the tube entering the crop.

Formerly this cramming was done by hand through a funnel, forcing eighty pounds of salty, fatty, cooked corn down the goose's throat. This has been compared to making a man eat twenty-eight pounds of spaghetti a day, so that he becomes horribly blown up and distended with violent liver pains, but must go on eating and eating although every forced mouthful aggravates his agony.

In an article in Paris, Henry Kahn wrote in *The People* of 18 February 1962:

> After twenty days of this torture, the poor goose is so distended that it can hardly move. It is in terrible pain; it can breathe only with diffi-culty. After twenty-five days of agony comes the merciful relief—the goose is killed. There is great excitement when it is cut open because no one can say to what size the liver will have swollen. Sometimes it will weigh two pounds—and the bigger the liver the more *pâté*...and profit.

Other short cuts to greater production are the injection of hormones into ewes to result in multiple births, and the crossing of Friesian cows with the larger Charollais breeds to give more beef. The old Hereford cross on the dairy herds was not yielding large enough joints. The French Charollais breeds used in draught work sired quicker-growing bull calves carrying larger hindquarter development, which is where the choice and expensive cuts of meat are situated. At first the introduction of this breed was banned, but test-tubes of semen were smuggled in, and after that the breeders never looked back. The bigger-haunched calves have resulted in difficult births for the dairy cows and the farming journals have been full of advice as to how best to overcome these calving difficulties, minimizing damage to the cow. Horrifying accounts of protracted parturition, even when traction assisted, were soon forgotten when the larger beef calves were bringing increasing profits.

More short cuts are on their way. It has been shown that a saving of three shillings and sixpence per hen can be made if they are fasted one day a week, so it has been found profitable by one agricultural experimental station to fast battery hens each Sunday. Ewes can be fed on the protein of dried poultry manure. The taste was unpalatable, and so chicory and molasses were added. Stress is the enemy of inten-sive farming, so aspirin is recommended as an additive to feeds.

After an enquiry about immature calves being exported to the Conti-nent, the Ministry of Agriculture set a weight minimum of two hundred pounds per calf for calves for export. This meant that at least their navels were dry before they left the farm. But when there was a further public outcry about white veal production in this country, farmers found they could recoup their losses and in fact earn a handsome profit by exporting their calves to be turned into veal on the Continent, and the weight limit was brought down to one hundred and ten pounds. As calves are not weighed individually but by the lorry-load, there is no check on individual animals, and most certainly newly born animals are being subjected to the stress of long journeys to support an industry which the British public have decided they do not approve of in their own country. One French buyer stated on the radio that he had just bought six hundred calves and could do with six thousand which he hoped he could come back for. It seems that we do not mind much what goes on as long as it is out of our sight.

Finally, the food we eat, if it is animal, has to be slaughtered. The methods vary from electrocution to the knife, from the poleaxe to the 'humane slaughter' of captive bolt pistol and pithing rod. Even in Britain protection of animals does not extend to national preferences for methods of killing, and minorities have their own slaughter-houses. In Jewish Kosher killing the animal is not previously stunned, but is 'cast' and then has its throat cut.

After the great 1967 outbreak of foot-and-mouth disease in the British Isles there was an enquiry into allegations that numbers of the hastily slaughtered animals were not properly killed and that many were still alive when buried in quicklime. The defence was that one hundred per cent efficiency was impossible under these special circum-stances of haste, overwork, etc. A successful humane slaughter consists in stunning by applying a captive bolt pistol to the forehead, when a metal bolt about four inches long and little larger than a cigarette is fired with scarcely any explosion. The animal falls at once, usually without a sound. The piercing or 'pithing rod', a foot in length, is pushed into the hole in the skull made by the bolt, which may cause a momentary spasm of the nervous system before the animal is dead. Properly done, this is a painless, humane end.

In Britain most slaughtermen work on piece rates per finished car-case. Generally speaking, this tends to make for quick and humane dispatch, but occasionally impatience results in unnecessarily rough handling and broken bones between the lairage and the place of killing.

In 1961 the Rev. Michael Fryer, founder of Crusade Against All Animal Cruelty, wrote a horrifying account of a visit to the Municipal Slaughterhouse at Newcastle-on-Tyne, with beasts slipping and falling in a welter of blood and offal. A noose of rope tightened about their necks, they were hauled bellowing with terror to meet their doom.

> The more it struggled the tighter became the noose, until its neck was squeezed and contracted under the rope to an unbelieveably small dimension. It appeared to be strangling and choking, so that it could only get its breath in whistling shrieks. Little by little they shortened the rope, shouting and swearing at the poor creature (they were losing money every moment it resisted their efforts) and drawing it inch by inch they pulled its head close to the floor.—A slaughterman again took the noose into the lairage, a shout and bloody hands began to pull and I watched the scene enacted over again. I was not alone. The other sightseers were local schoolchildren who came daily to 'enjoy the fun'.

As a result of this exposure, the Newcastle-upon-Tyne abattoir was rebuilt and the whole system improved. But many sub-standard slaughterhouses still remain even in our highly civilized and sophisticated western countries. The beatings, the blood and terror are still present, though usually well out of sight down back streets away from the gaze of the general public. That it is possible to slaughter humanely and cleanly was revealed by our visit to a bacon factory. The pigs were electrically stunned by a 250-volt charge in an atmosphere of clinical cleanliness and efficiency. It should not be impossible to deal with larger beasts in the same way. They have their lives taken away for our benefit, and we owe them as quick and terror-free an end as we can devise.

The pressure upon the slaughterhouse services may result in hasty work that cannot bother to check on the niceties of instant death or that all life has departed before the flaying hook or scalding tank is reached. It may also mean that the lairages are packed with waiting animals for whom there is no adequate attention and who must remain unfed and unwatered.

However, there are always people who will care, even about what they cannot see. In France it was the film star, Brigitte Bardot, who led a protest against inhumane slaughter and pressed for adoption of up-to-date methods. ISPA (the International Society for Protection of Animals) does its best to help, but as late as 1967 the central abattoir in Athens where two thousand animals each day were slaughtered possessed only one captive bolt pistol.

In Britain, there have been several attempts to bring slaughter in Jewish and Mohammedan abattoirs into line with the existing laws for humane killing.

In Britain the 1933 Act, specifying that animals should be stunned before having their throats cut, exempted the 200,000 or so beasts killed each year by Kosher or similar methods, although veterinary surgeons and slaughtermen testified that having throats cut in full consciousness can lead to suffering.

In 1968 Mr David Ensor, MP for Bury, made another attempt to secure for the growing number of beasts slaughtered by 'inhumane' methods the same kind of safeguards accorded meat animals for gentile consumption. The growing number of immigrants in our larger cities had led to poultry and horses being added to the 'ritual slaughter' victims and a good deal of disquiet was expressed by the general public when these cases were ventilated.

The Imam of the Shah Jehan Mosque in Woking told the Humane Slaughter Association that 'the use of a humane killer does not in any way go against the teaching of Islam'. But the Orthodox Jews would not give way and defended their slaughter methods with the statement that it had been ordained that to eat meat containing blood was forbidden. Yet it has been proved that it is impossible to drain a carcase completely of blood, even when it has been produced by the Kosher method. Indeed, the only way to be certain of not consuming any blood at all, would be to become vegetarian.

In Norway, Sweden, Switzerland and Upper Austria, it is now prohibited by law to kill any beast without first stunning it. In Britain, gentile slaughtermen could be prosecuted for failing to stun while under the same roofs Kosher killings can quite legally take place. The proposed bill has pointed out that Jewish customers consume only the forequarters of the beast killed while the remaining joints are sold on the general market. This means that gentile consumers may be eating Kosher-killed meat in the belief that their joint was produced 'humanely'.

In spite of this anomaly and the strength of public feeling, the bill did not receive a second reading. One of the reasons given was that it showed racial prejudice. Another less-publicized reason may have been one referred to by the late Robert Crouch, MP, himself a farmer, who in campaigning for the end of ritual slaughter discovered that one of the by-products was the blood which is manufactured into profitable commodities: the white corpuscles into albumen for chemical purposes and the haemoglobin into dried blood fertilizer. He found the forces of commerce too powerful for him to combat, even with the pressure of public opinion largely on his side. The Shechita Committee defend their slaughter methods by stating that, properly used, the knife renders death instantaneous. The opposition point to lesser animals, such as sheep, staggering about for some time after their throats have been cut, while the bigger animals, the cows and bullocks, suffer considerably in being forced into the narrow casting pen and then turned upside down, having their heads pulled through an aperture and their throats stretched prior to cutting. It is also maintained by Shechita critics that a certain amount of blood remains in the head to feed the brain and that consciousness lingers for some time after the knife has been used.

On the racial discrimination charge, many people pointed out that freedom to worship in their own way by minorities must yet be within certain limits in any civilized community. Human sacrifice and the practice of *suttee* were cited as once valid religious practices now commuted to something more acceptable in our time.

Whatever the arguments there is little doubt that, just as colliers have a saying that few would burn coal if they had to hew it, similarly there would be fewer meat-eaters if we all had to slaughter our own food.

# 8

# *Horsemeat*

'Nobility without pride, friendship without
envy, England's past has been born on his back.
All our history is his industry. We are his
heirs, he is our inheritance.'
RONALD DUNCAN'S TOAST 'THE HORSE'

The logical end of a horse is horsemeat, whether in pet food or for
human consumption. There is no moral reason to be more squeamish
about eating horse or pony than about eating cow or pig. There are,
however, certain aspects of the trade in horseflesh which are not
immediately apparent to the uncommitted onlooker. The remark of a
witness of a recent Dartmoor pony sale is a pointer: 'I am no more
against the slaughter of horses for meat than I am of sheep or cattle,
but after seeing the way they are handled en route and on the other
side (i.e. on the Continent) I am against them being *exported alive*.'

Horses are more nervous travellers than cattle and therefore more
capable of feeling distress and pain and of inflicting it upon one
another. Consignments of cattle tend to be of fairly uniform weight
and size, but a consignment of horses can vary enormously with quite
young foals in crowded transports with older, heavier animals, resulting in injury. We have witnessed examples of this. A tractor back-
firing may have little effect on a cow, which will simply go on chewing
the cud, while a pony will panic and try to bolt. Horses often struggle
more when being loaded, so inviting force and brutality. An animal
which has been a child's pet or has belonged to a household, used to
human company and regular attention, may well suffer more than
cattle on the long road to the abattoir.

Lastly and perhaps most important, as long sea journeys are all too
often involved—the horse with its muscular tight sphincter cannot
vomit and find relief in sea-sickness and consequently suffers agony.
Horses also need food 'little and often' and frequently need water. If
these are denied they suffer from an abdominal pain akin to acute

Dead animals for the exotic food market. (*Bernhard Juraczewski*)

*Above*
The picador's act. The second stage of the bullfight. Notice the gashes in the horse's padding. (*Syndication International, Daily Mirror*)

*Below*
A stag lies dead at the end of a hunt in the West Country of England.
(*Syndication International, Daily Mirror*)

indigestion in humans, resulting in grave discomfort and eventual collapse. Standing in dirt for longish periods brings about inflammation of the feet. British and Irish ponies and horses have been traced beyond the well-known markets and abattoirs of Holland, France and Belgium. In Italy, where meat dishes are expensive and good cuts scarce, it is very probable that some dishes appearing as veal on the menu are in fact young pony meat. Italy, with its large appetite for imported meat — Italian farming stresses arable cultivation rather than animal husbandry — imports live horses for slaughter from as far away as South America. The sufferings of horses on sea journeys of that length can best be imagined by noting that *The Guardian* of 15 April 1966 bore the headline '282 horses sent to Italy die before slaughter'. The account reads:

> *Il Corriere della Sera*, the Milan newspaper, disclosed these figures today, and any student of the situation is likely to set the true figure higher. The horses came from Brazil and Argentina and reached Italy in old cargo boats not specially equipped to transport live animals. Many of them were not accustomed to close confinement nor to dry fodder. They suffered from sea-sickness and panic, and most of the deaths were caused by malnutrition and trampling.
>
> A ship carrying four hundred and sixty two horses reached Genoa on November 22nd and the animals reached their final destination, Parma, two days later by rail. Twenty-four were dead when the customs seals on the vans were broken in Parma. They had made the rail journey without fodder or water in vans designed for transporting twelve animals, not the fifteen they were transporting.

In Britain we have seen transports so grossly overcrowded that the door had to be forced shut by the combined weight of men pushing against it. There are never enough inspectors of either the RSPCA or the police to interfere successfully at such times.

*The Guardian* goes on to state that 173 horses of the original Parma shipment were dead before slaughter, because the municipal slaughter-house was not equipped to shelter such a number all at once. So those which survived the journey from their native South American prairies, the long, rough sea journey, and then the transports without fodder or water, died of exhaustion and injury before they could become horsemeat. This seems a fantastic waste in every respect.

That horses, so ill-equipped for sea travel, are sent vast distances across the oceans of the world was brought home to us quite accidentally when we offered a lift to a seaman hitch-hiking back to his ship in Liverpool. We asked him if he enjoyed his work, and he revealed that for years he had been on the 'South American run' and would not exchange the life for any other. The only thing he disliked about it was the frequent carrying of 'polo ponies' between the Argentine and Liverpool.

Completely ignorant of our specialized interest in the subject, he talked freely and indignantly of horses left in the blazing sun on deck for days during loading and unloading, with no exercise and only dry fodder. One mare left on deck in Liverpool for weeks because of some hitch in the quarantine regulations had been hosed down to relieve her sufferings, but she could not lie down and had gone lame. We obtained the name of his ship and duly apprised the Liverpool RSPCA of this man's evidence, expressing the hope that they would keep this shipping line and its cargoes under observation. But when incidents like this come to light purely by accident it leads us to wonder how much suffering goes on unobserved and unreported because it is 'nobody's business'. Only extreme cases hit the headlines because they cannot be concealed, but the traffic continues with all its attendant suffering year after year because the buyers want animals on the hoof rather than the hook.

Recently in Australia the plight of the 'brumbies', the wild horses of the outback, rounded up and sent long distances by rail to be slaughtered for pet food, hit the headlines. Some of these animals had scarcely seen a human being and were not easily corralled and herded into rail wagons for journeys of hundreds of miles. Many of them died on the way, and many more were injured. Humane societies made representations, stock trains were limited to a maximum speed of sixty miles per hour, and a campaign to supply fodder and water at least at destination point was set afoot. The mortality rate was greatly reduced.

In the summer of 1966 the spotlight turned on Canada when it was revealed that horses sent from the logging camps in the woods of New Brunswick were arriving at Quebec abattoirs in distressing condition. The Canadian Society for the Prevention of Cruelty to Animals stated that upwards of 45,000 horses were used in the timber industry of Eastern Canada and that humane inspection and control were long overdue. A thousand 'forest' horses a year leave the lumber camps for abattoirs in Quebec, which also absorb an additional 4,000 horses from Ontario. The condition of many of these animals, destined for the meat trade after a life of hard labour, was so pitiful that the Department of Natural Resources promised to take action. The Canadian SPCA, reporting some small improvements in conditions, added:

> We achieved this improvement by making representation to the horse dealers concerned, the federal government, the provincial govern-

ment and the slaughter house. We do not feel that the situation is ideal by any means; but the improvement is encouraging. It must be emphasized, however, that it is comparatively simple to spot ill-treatment of horses while they are in transit. But horses are still ill-treated in the woods. All we have done is to deal with that part of the iceberg showing. We are doing what we can with the remaining and larger area, but with inadequate funds and too few inspectors we are severely hampered in our efforts.

Most pony and horse meat in Britain goes into pet food, because as a nation we have an aversion to horsemeat for human consumption. About 100,000 tons of horsemeat is eaten in France alone each year. The abattoir at Vaugirard slaughters 2,000 horses each week, and a great number of families depend on this trade for their livelihood. Other continental countries, particularly Italy, have similar appetites for horseflesh, which Great Britain and Ireland help to supply.

Many surplus ponies go from Britain under licence to Holland and Belgium for riding, but these countries, too, are reaching saturation point when it comes to pets. Continental dealers and butchers, always used to handling larger quantities of horseflesh than their British counterparts for the meat trade, find that even after paying 'riding' prices there is still a profit to be made, and afterwards the hide goes as 'ponyskin', a popular fur in Dutch and Belgian stores.

The horse-market at Hedel in Holland clears up to 3,000 horses and ponies a year, many of the ponies from Dartmoor. Mrs Doris Lock, an energetic representative of the Dartmoor Livestock Protection Society (formed after the severe winter of 1963-4, when it was estimated that scores of ponies were frozen or starved to death on Dartmoor alone), has stated that butchers and slaughter-men from Germany, Belgium, France and even Italy are present at these sales.

In 1967 ponies fetched an average of about sixty pounds apiece, and if this seems a high price, consider that to buy anything worth riding in this country something from eighty to a hundred pounds must be paid (for a non-pedigree animal).

On the Continent the price of meat is higher than in this country. Many ponies are small-boned but still carry a high percentage of useful meat and, of course, by-products. Even when the animal has been exported ostensibly for riding, there may be as much as a twenty-pound profit margin in turning it into meat. Continental suppliers know that they will see their money back.

On 1 October 1967 Mr Robert Porter, for the *Sunday Telegraph*, wrote an account of a journey he made to Belgium and Holland following the 'ponies for meat' trail. Before setting out he had found a guarded, even hostile, attitude on the part of most officials, and concluded that as a nation we are very touchy about allegations of how we exploit horses. Mr Porter went to Amsterdam and on to a well-known pony sale at the village of Heeton, near Deventer.

Mrs Lock and three other members of the Dartmoor Livestock Protection Society had arrived previously. All had plenty of experience of the various pony breeds and of brand marks, and knew what to look for. They identified dozens of animals from Britain, some with metal tags revealing that they had come from Great Yarmouth to Holland via Scherevingen.

There were Welsh ponies and Shetlands in addition to the Dartmoors, some of the handlers were drunk, and a small Shetland which had collapsed was kicked to its feet by a man wearing heavy wooden sabots. Mrs Lock herself received rough treatment when she gave water to some of the animals.

The women bought one pony which they considered to be in too pitiful a state to travel further, and it was given grazing by a Roman Catholic priest, Father Van Hoesel, in a field next to his church. The local veterinary surgeon, Mr Johannes Kemna, stated that it was too young to be on sale, most certainly should not be moved further, and needed rest for a week with care and warmth. This same vet, when asked about the fate of the ponies for sale, stated that some were slaughtered by local butchers and some went to Dutch pony clubs. He finished with the words: 'There are dealers here from the whole of the Netherlands and Germany. Young Irish pony meat is a favourite delicacy, but some of the meat is pickled and seasoned.'

Robert Porter's article stated that more than 1,000 ponies were sold at the Heeton pony sale that day. One dealer said he bought ponies from all over Europe including the United Kingdom, and that young pony meat would fetch upwards of fifteen shillings per pound.

Unsold ponies from Heeton were driven back into lorries and taken further afield to other markets, where their ordeal would begin all over again. So much transporation under far from ideal conditions has led observers to comment that many of these animals can hardly move when they arrive at their ultimate destination. Some of the crowded lorries ply between markets and the German border, sometimes over it (judging from the names and addresses noted on butchers' vans).

On 8 May 1967 a prominently featured item in *The Times* described the appalling conditions under which fourteen unbroken ponies were transported at speeds of up to seventy miles per hour over the Belgian cobbles to a slaughterhouse at Rance near the French border. The ponies, some in foal, were loaded on to a ferry at Dover on 19 April and went via Zeebruge. They were followed by three British investigators, who alleged that during the entire journey the animals had had no fodder or water. Mr John Pardoe, MP for Cornwall North, a man interested in the problem of humane treatment for live exports, stated that some people responsible for exporting ponies were undoubtedly breaking the law. The investigators, who included a retired Ministry of Transport supervising examiner, were told in Rance that a property owner in the village imported hundreds of foreign ponies. An official source in Brussels disclosed, when pressed, that only a few of the large number of imported ponies ended up in riding schools or as pets.

In September 1968 the *Sunday Telegraph* made a further attempt to expose the pony-meat trade to the Continent and printed their findings in a very explicit feature by R. Barry O'Brien, a special correspondent reporting from Antwerp. He insisted that ponies exported as children's pets were going for slaughter instead. He quoted a Belgian dealer as having said to him 'I like to buy the little Welsh ponies from the pits. They are the most tasty. Dartmoor and Shetland are also good, but small for the money.'

It is salutory to note that after the press exposures of the pony trade the Ministry of Agriculture once more announced that the evidence was 'not sufficient basis on which they could suspend pony exports and hold an enquiry'. One reason for this attitude would appear to be that ponies are officially exported for breeding and riding so that, on paper, 'meat' ponies do not exist. But a Continental butcher with cash in hand is not going to enquire for what object the horse was originally exported.

Humane-thinking people on and around Dartmoor are not the only defenders of our indigenous horses against unnecessary suffering. The New Forest Society was originally started for the protection of all New Forest animals and with the special aim of preventing road accidents and loss of life, both human and animal, on the New Forest roads. The Hon. Secretary, Mrs J. Westren, who lives in the heart of the Forest south-west of Southampton, has fought long and tenaciously for better conditions. She and her helpers campaigned against unnecessarily cruel branding, sometimes done so badly that the burnt skin sloughed off completely so that the animal had to be branded again. Above all, for years this Society has been campaigning against the export of their local ponies to the Continent for meat. One or two convictions on a technicality have been obtained concerning the breaking of Forest bye-laws, with the offender being fined a paltry few pounds which could soon be recouped on this remunerative traffic.

The main victory of the New Forest Society has been in pressing for the adequate fencing of all trunk roads through the forest. In spite of this having gone ahead over a period of years, one of the main roads between Southampton and Bournemouth is still not adequately protected. The police figure for motorists involved in accidents with Forest animals between 1962 and 1966 was 1,439. As late as 1967 140 ponies were killed and 31 injured on the Forest roads. Many of these accidents happen at night with veterinary help not readily available, and the toll of suffering is immense, although gradually diminishing.

With the fencing of the roads, the grazing becomes less free and animals are contained within smaller areas, which affects the number of stock the Forest can comfortably carry and means that in hard times some of the horses and ponies may have to be farmed out elsewhere. But, having discovered the value of horses as a cash crop and ready form of export commodity, dealers and graziers are loathe to relinquish their profits and are out to exploit every possibility of the trade. Furthermore, farmers are exhorted to export as much as possible to help the national economy, and this traffic in horses is not likely to diminish for some time. The figure of 10,000 a year is given for the near future, for if the demand for riding horses should fall the market for horsemeat will remain constant, since it is cheaper than beef.

One problem is that Continental markets want the use of the hide, horsehair, and hoof—in fact, the whole carcass, not just the meat. The by-products can be manufactured into acceptable goods for export back to the country of the ponies' origin.

Between the two world wars there was an outcry against the export of worn-out work horses to the Continent, particularly Belgium. As far back as 1910 legislation was attempted to stop this kind of traffic, but an animal that had ceased to give any further service to its owners could still fetch a pound or two more by being despatched to countries which would pay for horsemeat. The agitation blew up again in the 1920s, and various humane people raised campaigns to obtain better conditions of transport and to obtain regulations governing the age and fitness of the animals exported. As work horses gave way to tractors on our farms and motor transport on our roads, the scandal of horse traffic died out in the popular press and in the minds of the general public, only to be revived with tremendous impact in the 1950s when the *City of Waterford* sailed from Cork to Dieppe in bad weather and jettisoned about sixty of its cargo of horses destined for slaughter.

The indignation switched to Ireland had some effect, but might never have come to light if the carcasses (their legs tied together) had not been washed ashore on the coast of Pembrokeshire, in Wales. Veterinary authorities stated that, unable to be 'seasick', these horses had died in agony from the effects of the rough weather. The captain and crew of the *City of Waterford* declared that they had done all in their power to save their live cargo. This did not prevent other horse boats from sailing, but, as a result of demonstrations on the docks at Dublin, Cork and elsewhere in Eire, and of the public outcry which attended the revelations of this trade, the Irish Horse Abattoir Investment Company was formed, so that horses might be slaughtered in Ireland and so be saved the sea journey. This concern was started by a board of women directors in 1959, largely from public subscription in both Eire and Britain. Belgian experts were called in to train the Irish workers, licences for 'humane consumption' were granted, and self-refrigerating containers were bought to comply with the Continental marketing regulations. The directors planned the layout of abattoir, waiting fields, and collecting pens to minimize suffering, and in spite of such 'expensive refinements' the project paid, which shows what can be done.

In spite of its success, this venture has not entirely eliminated the traffic in horses, ponies, and donkeys from Eire to the Continent. Because of the national outcry, an age limit was fixed: animals for export must be not more than seven years old. This was later reduced to five. With this limit being enforced, there was a noticeable rise in the number of horses exported as 'working' animals, rather than for meat, until the anomalous situation arose in which old horses with just a little working life left in them could be exported while those just over the age limit could not. It seems that loop-holes can be found in every law aimed to protect animals and that commercial interests very soon discover ways round regulations aimed at cutting profitable trading. In the first six months that the age limit was reduced to five years, 13,000 'working horses', each averaging sixty pounds in value, were exported!

Eire still continues to export horses, ponies and donkeys to this country and to the Continent, but at least the traffic has been brought out into the open and no one concerned can plead ignorance of the conditions under which these animals travel, nor of the fate for which they are intended.

# 9

## *The Luxury Business*

'Leopard skins look best on leopards.'
PETER SCOTT

Furs are one of the ultimate luxuries of the world, like jewels. They have a voluptuous beauty of their own. Every Snow Queen in fairy-tale imagination should be lapped in white ermine; every Prince Charming splendid in Russian sables. What is the commercial reality behind this dream?

Thirty million wild animals are killed yearly, for the value of their skins alone. Most are killed by trapping. The traps are of the 'gin' variety, sometimes referred to as leg-hold or steel-toothed traps. 'If all these millions could be gathered together in one place, they would make with their broken and outraged bodies, their sunken eyes and frozen faces, a mountain of death that would terrify...' wrote Professor Howard Moore, Instructor of Zoology at Chicago. Frank Conibear, an ex-trapper of thirty-two years' experience, describes two of the minks he found in his traps, set two weeks previously:

> In the first trap we find a mink's foot. The area about the trap is all bashed about and chewed up by the mink in its effort to escape. The mink is a tough animal that struggles, attempting by jerks and pulls to get loose. It writhes and twists desperately. After a time, from the pressure of the jaws of the trap, and the swelling of the leg from pain, the circulation of blood stops, and the foot becomes numb, but the pain above it in the swollen leg and shoulder must increase and the mink must be in agony. The foot will freeze. This may be in a few hours or a day, depending mostly on the weather. After the foot becomes numb or frozen, the mink, desperately savage with pain, will chew at it. Sometimes it will chew the toes off underneath the jaws of the trap and be able to pull the foot out. At other times it will chew at the leg itself... and by chewing and twisting will, (if it does not freeze to death first)

sometimes after several days, especially if the bone has been broken, sever the last sinew holding the leg and foot together and escape.

In the next mink trap visited, the mink is dead. It is stretched out as it threw itself in the last spasm and frozen hard and stiff. The fur is fine and glossy; it will make some woman a lovely neckpiece.

The trapper said that this mink lived three or four days.

The foot is lacerated, swollen and covered with blood. The stump of the leg above the trap is swollen four times its normal size. The shoulder too is all swollen. When we skin it, we will find that all the area will be a mass of blood-coloured, sticky gelatine-like substance, indicating the terrible suffering it had gone through before death released it. The trap is slowly severing the last shred of sinews.

Most people living in great urban areas have probably never heard the agonized screams of a wild creature caught in a trap. This anguish in the night, in the remote wastes and forests of the world, on the shores of civilization, is something too far removed from the sort of lives most of us lead.

However, countryfolk will recall nights before myxomatosis decimated the rabbit population of this country, when rabbit trappers visited their gin-traps, the nights filled with tormented squealing.

The Scott-Henderson Committee reported: 'The gin-trap is a diabolical instrument which causes an incalculable amount of pain', and recommended that it should be banned, but did not recommend that gin-traps should be called in. People comfort themselves with thinking that the gin-trap is now illegal in England and Wales, and will be soon in Scotland (in 1973); but it is still in use in many other countries, and particularly in the countries which produce the bulk of wild furs. And Great Britain still manufactures and exports steel-toothed traps. In a reply to Mr Hugh Jenkins, who had asked if steps would be taken to prohibit the manufacture for export of these traps, the President of the Board of Trade said that the Board had no general powers to prohibit the manufacture of goods for sale in the home market or for export.

Trappers claim to lose about one third of animals caught in steel-toothed, 'leghold' gin-traps, because they chew off paw, foot, or toes. The traplines, being often far away from base, may be visited only once a week or less; and so, once caught, the animals linger for days in agony, slowly dying of cramp, thirst and starvation, suffering, exposure, exhaustion and attack, often frozen to death, until the trappers at last return to finish off the survivors.

Canadian trappers use steel traps, of many designs and sizes, to capture thirty-six different kinds of mammals – muskrats and squirrells, badgers, coyotes, foxes, weasels, martens, bears. Canada has few laws on the use of steel traps, except restrictions as to places and periods for trapping. Yet the Canadian Society for the Prevention of Cruelty to Animals believes that there is at present much cruelty in the trapping of wild animals.

The Universities Federation for Animal Welfare, too, has come out very strongly against fur trapping methods, and their technical secretary, F. J. Vintner, has compiled a very telling if saddening booklet, *Facts About Furs*.

The booklet comments:

> All sorts of animals get trapped, valuable ones and worthless ones, predators and domestic pets, the right ones and the wrong ones, the immature and the pregnant, the trap does not discriminate.

Quoting J. R. Baker on *The Scientific Basis of Kindness to Animals*, the UFAW booklet continues:

> If you want a rough idea of the leghold trap, just imagine that the door of your car has been slammed across the fingers of your bare hand. Imagine that the door is jammed shut and imagine that you are then left with your hand so caught until you either starve to death or freeze to death or tear your hand apart.

The cost of a fur coat, when reckoned in animal suffering, is prohibitive, when one imagines a fox – an animal as large and well-developed as a pet dog – caught by the leg until it dies of hunger or thirst. And how can one assess the price of a beaver skin whose former owner chewed off a paw in an effort to escape the biting steel, only to be recaught on its remaining legs?

North American trappers, to prevent loss by foot chewing – known as a 'wring-off' – have developed the 'jump trap' which catches the animal higher up the leg. Stop-loss, double-jaw and two-trigger traps are aimed at a second grip of the animal so that it cannot struggle and bite free. The initial impact of the animal's paw on the 'plate' springs the trap in the usual way, but a second set of steel jaws then closes on the main part of the body. This reduces the number of animals who cheat the trappers, but it is doubtful if it is more humane.

But probably the greatest barbarity is meted out to the little animal whose skin is the most noble and regal of all, the ermine. The price of each skin is about a pound. Four hundred ermine skin are needed for one Coronation robe. The skin is too precious to risk any damage occurring to it in a trap, so iron bars are smeared with grease. The grease attracts the ermine, which licks it. The intense cold on the iron makes the ermine's tongue freeze fast to the bars, 'as if it had been put into a vice'. Professor Howard Moore, Instructor of Zoology at Chicago, reports:

> There is no possibility of escape, except by pulling the tongue out by the roots. The inevitable struggles to escape cause a larger and larger area to become adherent to the pitiless iron, and in time the whole mouth region may become solidified from the prolonged exposure in the bitter Arctic cold.

The organizers of Canada's annual seal slaughter say that bad publicity is ruining their business. If by bad publicity they mean showing and telling exactly how white-coated baby seals are bashed to death, then it had better be shown and told over and over again, so that the best-dresser skiing down the slopes, the lady chairman on the platform, the well-heeled customer at the exclusive furrier shall know exactly what is being done on her behalf. In every baby seal fur coat there are between five and eight skins that have been peeled off these baby animals. Sometimes they are dead, and sometimes, according to observers, they are still alive.

Reports of the Farne Island 'cullings' (or killings, to drop a euphemism of 1964) led to public unease over the cruelties inherent in the methods of the sealing industry. Public protests continued, in Canada and in Britain, and observers from humane societies researched and reported on the methods of the hunt. The Secretary of the New Brunswick SPCA reported:

> Horrible as it is, the baby seal being skinned alive is only part of the cruelty of seal hunting. Adult seals are shot and many escape to die a lingering and painful death beneath the ice…We must also consider the evident horror of many of the animals as they are hunted down. We have seen baby seals 'play dead', run, scream, urinate, defecate, or even pathetically try to fight back. We have seen the anguish of mother seals watching their young being butchered alive. I have seen living animals being crushed by steel-hulled ships as these same ships cut their way through the living herds.

An article in *With Sword and Shield*, headed 'Piece workers do not give themselves time to kill painlessly' said:

> The gangs of hunters are only hired for a short period in the slaughtering season, they usually consist of uneducated, easily available, unemployed, who work on piece work and in competition, and are paid by the skin…Since it has become easier by the use of light aircraft to visit the seal hunters, at least in the Gulf of St. Lawrence, press and cameramen have frequently in recent years been witnesses of this

slaughter. Cameramen and animal conservationists now saw with horror that to no small extent the little animals were still alive and trying to defend themselves while they were being skinned. This is partly due to the lack of skill of the slaughterers and the fact that they quickly become callous, and partly to the haste with which they skin the animals on shifting ice and in bad weather conditions in the intense cold, and under the need to obtain the greatest number in a day.

A report, 'Sealing in UK and Canadian Waters', made by I. L. Hughes at a symposium on sealing organized by the Universities Federation for Animal Welfare, had much the same to say:

> Some airborne sealers did not bother to carry any form of club at all but instead simply flipped the young seals over and slashed them with a longitudinal cut of the throat. Others merely kicked the young seals in the head with their heavy boots with the intention, presumably, of stunning them. I saw a number of young seals that had been kicked in this way that had suffered serious injury, but which were conscious and capable of movement and of noise.

The *Sunday Times* magazine of 3 September 1967 published a report by Mr A. G. Bourne, FLS, FRGS, a marine biologist, specialist in sealing and whaling industries, member of the Council of the Association of British Zoologists and of the Scientific Committee of the Field Studies Council. He wrote:

> After examining the hunt as widely as possible and observing all the information we could gather, we concluded there was a great deal of cruelty, most of it quite unnecessary, due in the main to carelessness and fatigue.

Dr Elizabeth Simpson, Professor of Pathology at the University of Cambridge, was present at the hunting and carried out post-mortems on hundreds of seal bodies. Her conclusions were that thirty-six per cent of the 185,000 baby seals killed each year in the Gulf of St Lawrence and other Canadian sealing grounds are skinned alive, and that most of these are nurselings of less than four weeks old.

It is not only the methods used which cause concern, but the possibility of oversealing, especially the threatened extinction of individual herds of harp seals.

Various species have disappeared or have become very rare already, particularly the fur-bearing Japanese sea-lion, and the Galapagos and Guadalupe fur seals. The legal limit for killing harp seals is 50,000 a year, but in reality many more are slaughtered. The population in the Newfoundland area has fallen more rapidly than that in the Gulf of St

Lawrence, owing to heavy additional catches of moulting adults, or immature animals. Together the population of the Gulf and Newfoundland areas has dropped by about half in fourteen years.

In 1969 the outcry against seal slaughter continued. *Paris Match* condemned sealing and it was stated that they influenced the Canadian Minister of Agriculture to visit the scenes of the massacre for himself. The Minister declared that 'there was a real concern from a conservation point of view over the seal situation in the Gulf of St Lawrence' and the slaying was halted when 35,000 baby seals had been killed. Only 250,000 seals remained, compared with the normal reproducing population of 750,000, and no more than 6,000 baby seals remained after the annual hunt. The survivors may seem numerous enough to the layman, but as so many more were killed, it is plain that the rate of sealing cannot be kept up without exterminating the seals altogether.

Many baby seals die, even if they escape the seal killers, being run down by ships or drowned when icefloes break up, as they are helpless until three or four weeks old.

In 1968 *The Times* showed a picture of more than five hundred leopard skins from Africa on display by a Paris importer. The choicest skins were stated to be worth more than one thousand pounds each. One of *The Times* readers who wrote in to the newspaper after this photograph was Peter Scott, who pointed out that for this display of selected skins many more than five thousand lepards would have perished, and that the fashion for spotted furs is bringing a number of large cat species near to extinction. He concluded his letter with the slogan 'Leopard skins look best on leopards'.

Another victim of fashion and trend-setting is the vicuna, a small wild type of llama inhabiting the high Andes of Peru and Bolivia. This is becoming another threatened animal, since its high-quality wool has become popular. Britain is one of the leading importers of the fibre manufactured from vicuna wool which sells at sixty-five pounds per square yard. Although now officially protected in Peru, the vicuna is endangered by vast smuggling and poaching activities.

Señor Felipe Benavides, President of the National Parks of Peru, has asked the British Government to ban its imports of vicuna cloth, urging that we write to the World Wildlife Fund and our Members of Parliament demanding action. He expressed the hope that other European countries might then follow Britain's example. He points out that although there were 2,000,000 vicunas at the turn of the century there are no more than 10,000 left today. Calling a halt to the killing would give time for rational plans to be introduced for recovering the wool without destroying the animal and to enable the herds to re-establish themselves. But if Peru discusses preservation, Bolivia turns a blind eye to the consequences of ruthless slaughter and imposes no restrictions whatever on the export of wool, even though the vicunas are mown down by machine-guns on their ranging territories near Mount Sajama in the Oruro district.

The vicuna could therefore suffer the fate of the chinchilla, whose skin was so greatly prized that even as far back as the 1900s European furriers marketed wild chinchilla coats for the staggering sum of twenty-five thousand pounds each. 'The wanton destruction of the world's stocks of wild chinchillas reveals furriers as among the worst, most deliberately and short-sightedly greedy of all exploiters of natural animal populations', wrote Richard Fitter in *Vanishing Wild Animals of the World*, discussing species after species that have been wiped from the face of the world, or brought to the very brink of extermination, by man's insatiable greed and vanity. One of these was the Koala bear, which was very nearly exterminated after being slaughtered by the million for its pelt.

In the long run it is the consumer who creates the demand and who is, in the last resort, culpable. The *Daily Mail* of 28 October 1968 carried a caption 'The Rarest Coat in the World', over a picture of Mrs Hazel Lyon wearing a Bengal tigerskin coat. According to the *Daily Mail* Mrs Lyon said she felt very proud. 'I feel I've achieved something' she was quoted as saying. The Bengal, Manchurian, Chinese, Javan, Sumatran and Caspian tiger are all decreasing at an alarming rate, while the Bali tiger is stated to be already on the verge of extinction.

The skins of snakes, lizards and other reptiles are obtained by nailing them alive through the head to a tree or post; a slit is then cut in the back of the head and the whole skin pulled off in one piece. Dr Felix Kropstein, who practised medicine for a number of years in Indonesia says that many hundreds of thousands of large and small skins are brought annually to the skin markets of the Sunda Islands, and the water snake, about ten feet long, is caught in enormous numbers in Borneo. After skinning the creatures no one cares further about them, although days may pass before death ends their tortures. In the French periodical, *Sciences et Voyages*, a report appeared from R. Thevinin, which is confirmed by Dr Kropstein, concerning the skinning alive of giant snakes.

The snake is suspended in space, with no support whatever on which to exert its strength, between a rope round the head lashed to a tree, and a helper pulling at the tail end. Like this, even a powerful python several yards in length can be held by one person. The skin is split and pulled off as if the living creature is being unzipped.

Flies and ants then torment the skinless animal with bites and stings until, after several days, the bleeding body hangs lifeless, with insects crawling all over it. Meanwhile its handsome skin has been carried off to make a chain of substantial profits, and to end up as prized shoes, handbag or wallet.

The Beauty Without Cruelty Movement, under the presidency of the late Air Chief Marshall Lord Dowding, gave wide publicity to the many abuses and cruelties used in other products with which we pamper and glamorize ourselves.

Civet musk is reportedly one of the twenty most important raw materials used in the perfume industry and the basis of a flourishing trade between the Ethiopian producers and the French perfume market, although some famous perfumiers both in France and in this country now use a substitute as fixative agent.

The civet is an animal similar to a mongoose, striped or spotted, and three very rare types inhabit South-East Asia. But those trapped for the perfume industry are caught mainly in south-west Ethiopia for sale to civet farmers, who confine them in cages about three feet long and only eighteen inches high and wide, so that the cat can only move a short distance backwards and forwards and can barely turn round. Usually fifty such cages are crammed into a concrete shed with a corrugated tin roof, shuttered windows and closed doors. Fires are lit in the sheds to create a thick, smoky atmosphere. The temperature is maintained at about 110 degrees F. In these cramped, inhuman conditions, the cat must remain for the whole of its life span. In the wild, the civet will live about ten years; caged and tormented, it may last but half that time. When the cat is baited and enraged and fed on raw meat, it will excrete more musk.

Highest quality musk is obtained from the pouch of the male civet on the ventral face of the genital organ. The legs of the cat held apart, the musk pouch is opened by hand, and the musk is scraped off with a horn spatula, causing much pain and distress. The International Society for the Protection of Animals believes that 'this business subjects animals to totally unnecessary suffering, especially as good perfumes are now made with substitute fixative'. The Beauty Without Cruelty Movement has developed ranges of creams, soaps, and cosmetics in which no painful animal experimentation and no cruel processes have been involved.

The whale is one more animal whose products, spermaceti and ambergris, are universally and basically used in the beauty-cream, cosmetic, hairdressing and perfume industries. But the whale's plight and the barbarity of its killing have not aroused the protest and indignation they deserve. Commander Ommaney, RN (Ret.), formerly a government inspector in a British whale factory-ship, has said: 'Anything that can be done to educate public opinion about whaling is certainly a worthwhile job'.

Of all the animals afflicted by the ingenious, not to say diabolical, methods which man has invented for catching, hunting or killing them only the whale can claim the distinction of being deliberately 'blown up' internally by repeated charges of explosive. The harpoon, weighing about 1 cwt, has a head fitted with a grenade and a time-fuse to detonate. It also has prongs which expand inside the whale, like an opening umbrella, as the cable tightens. The damage caused by the shrapnel is very widespread, and great patches of blood stain the sea crimson.

Captain W. R. D. McLaughlin, who was with the well-known whaling firm of Salvesen of Leith for twenty-three years, and for fifteen of them was an officer with whaling factory-ships, wrote in his book, *Call to the South*:

> The first harpoon rarely kills. Two, three, up to six harpoons have to be used before some animals die. The whaleboat lies to a taut line, the whale nearly a mile away, somewhere out ahead still fighting, pulling with a force as powerful as a locomotive. As it tries to dislodge the harpoon from its body it tears itself to pieces. Slowly it dies a cruel death.

And Dr Harry R. Lillie, who went on a whaling expedition as ship's surgeon in 1946, wrote: 'A heavy bang. The harpoon flies out with a foregoer rope snaking behind in a falling arc. A horrible slap as the 150 lb weapon disappears in the creature's side, is followed in a couple of seconds by a dull thud as the explosive lacerates the intestines'. Dr Lillie says that the struggle may go on for an hour or more, while more harpoons are fired into the victim. 'I have seen nine harpoons used before the crippled creature's spouting, after five hours, subsided at last in a bubbling of blood as she died. A big Blue Whale far advanced in pregnancy. She had done all she could'. Standards of whale gunnery vary greatly; first class gunners may earn £4,000–£5,000 in the three-month season.

Richard Fitter in his *Vanishing Wild Animals of the World* wrote:

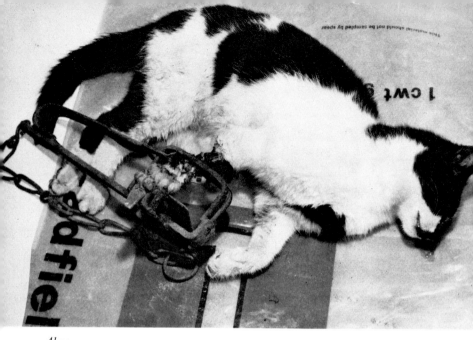

*Above*
A cat caught in a gin-trap. The animal had to be destroyed.

(*Suffolk Constabulary*)

*Below*
Greyhound coursing. In this picture, which depicts a Waterloo Cup incident,
two hounds are seen destroying a live hare.

(*Syndication International, Daily Mirror*)

The history of whaling has been one long disgraceful story of undisciplined greed among so-called civilised nations...All eight forms of whale at present on the danger list are baleen whales, for these are the commercially valuable ones, and all have been decimated entirely by man.

In an article in *The Observer* or 3 July 1966, Anne Taylor wrote:

The world's whaling industry appeared to cut its own throat in London last week. Next season's Antarctic catch was again fixed well above the level necessary if the fast dwindling population of the world's last great whaling ground is to survive...The World Wildlife Fund estimates that there were 30,000 blue whales in the Antarctic before the War; there are now about 600. There are so few whales left in the Atlantic grounds that factory ships are uneconomic there.

The blue whale which was once numerous has been reduced to a few hundred, because the necessary preservation quotas were not imposed by the whaling nations when the time was ripe. The grey whale stocks were brought to the verge of annihilation during the 1920s. The fin and sei whale population has been seriously depleted in spite of continuous warnings by scientists to the International Whaling Committee that quotas were too high. This insensate extermination of stocks is a barbarity as great as the methods of slaughter used in whaling.

All of which is succinctly summed up in a comment from John Davy in the *Observer* of 9 May 1965: 'If there were a prize for the world's most short-sighted industry, Antarctic Whaling would get it.'

In 1958 the United Nations Conference on the Law of the Sea requested states to prescribe by all means available to them those methods for the capture and killing of marine life, especially whales and seals, which will spare them suffering to the greatest possible extent.

The Russians have successfully experimented with the use on whale harpoons of curare, a South American poison, to replace explosives. Whales killed by explosives sink before they can be towed off, whereas curare is said to induce anaesthesia, so that the whales remain floating until it is convenient to pick them up. Curare may in fact not anaesthetise, but only paralyse—in which case it would not need a vivid imagination to guess at the suffering slow death of whales, in full consciousness.

Dr Lillie, who has seen the magnificent whales swimming at close quarters, says it is a thrilling sight: over one hundred tons in an eighty-foot length, the biggest mammal the earth has ever known, with its tongue alone weighing as much as an elephant, the poetry of majestic motion. 'A school of these creatures makes you feel that man has every reason to be humble'.

## 10

# *Beasts of Burden*

'I am an ass indeed;...I have served him from the hour of my nativity to this instant, and I have nothing at his hands for my service but blows. When I am cold, he heats me with beating; I am naked with it when I sleep; raised with it when I sit.'

'COMEDY OF ERRORS', SHAKESPEARE

Shakespeare wrote this about beasts of burden in the sixteenth century, and it could still hold equally true today in many countries and parts of the world.

From the ancient Camel caravans of the East, and the oxen bowed under the yoke ploughing the land in Biblical times right through to the twentieth century, draught animals can be considered as the very bones upon which the entire structure of civilization rests. These animals that have carried goods, to enable trade and industry to expand beyond primitive barter, that have built roads to build towns, have ploughed the land and heaved the loads which has made man's survival possible, have literally carried on their backs the whole emancipation and progress of man. Without them he would still be living the most primitive of existences. Therefore, mankind owes to these 'beasts of burden' the vast debt of his historical 'progress': Shakespeare knew how mankind has repaid it.

A. Picheng Lee, a Malayan writer, observed in 1948 that beasts of burden, such as horses, bullocks, donkeys, asses, elephants, camels etc. should be named 'the sub-human labourers'.

Although they are only animals, they perform human beings' tasks. They are practically regular labourers, most obedient, and never rebel against their masters. They receive no wages, are often over-worked and underfed, and finally they are murdered...A human labourer costs you more money and gives you more trouble in raising disputes which are frequently unfair towards you. A sub-human labourer costs you nothing except food and shelter, and in serving you obediently for life is superior to a human labourer. Yet the profit *you* derive and the treatment *they* receive are quite disproportionate. There is nothing more unjust and unscrupulous than this in the world.

One of the most disillusioning aspects of this particular branch of animal suffering is that even though man in relatively primitive conditions, with the twin-burdens of ignorance and poverty to hold him back, is thought to be progressing, the treatment to draught animals has ameliorated very little indeed; and any improvements have not generally stemmed from within, but have been achieved by efforts, pressures and persuasions of organizations from outside.

Unless entirely scrapped by increasing mechanization, the remaining draught animals suffer additional hazards and distress in semi-mechanized countries and cities where the level of driving consideration, road conduct, and vehicle road-worthiness is extremely low. This is probably particularly applicable to the countries of the near and far East.

As far as can be discovered, so the Organization of the Anglo-East European Fund states, there appears to be no organized animal welfare in Rumania and Bulgaria. Last year Government permission was secured to re-start the Hungarian SPCA, but it will be a very long time before effective organization and help can reach out to the most needed areas.

Czechoslovakia is an associate member of the world Federation for the Protection of Animals and has official Game, Fishery and other protection laws, of which precise details are difficult to obtain.

The Soviet Union officially pays regard to animal welfare. Popular imagination in the West conjures up pictures of vast, highly-mechanized collectives. This picture is partially true only, as there are equally vast numbers of smaller farms, even small-holdings, and animals, working in haulage and agriculture, and some of them to be seen about the countryside differ little from the poor-looking, meagre creatures common in Rumania, Hungary and Bulgaria. Enquiries do not reveal conclusive evidence of the incidence of vets, clinics, drugs and facilities, but by inference they are spread thinly.

As for Yugoslavia, where so much excellent work has been done in so many human domains, no provision seems to have been made for animal welfare. There are many extremely decrepit horses working on farms, and pulling the long heavy carts crammed with merchandise, and perhaps also an entire peasant family. Sometimes complete derelicts, appearing near to death, with foot infections, fistulous withers, harness galls, wounds, emaciation and colic are to be seen, particularly at country fairs and markets.

Probably more draught and working farm horses per capita, some 3,000,000, are to be seen in the Polish countryside, than anywhere else in Europe. The Anglo-East European Fund observes that animal welfare in Poland is advanced in some respects and that a progressive attitude on the part of the Government prevails although most of the horses are of a thin, light-type, seemingly unsuited for heavy farmwork in the very muddy conditions so often prevailing, especially after the thawing of the winter frosts. They appeared to us reasonably well-cared for, although most drivers carry a heavy stick, and these horses being the only equine breadwinner on these Polish small-holdings may certainly be worked to capacity or beyond.

It may also be said that a crucial shortage of good fodder, drugs, veterinary surgeons, or even competent farriers, and an almost total absence of animal clinics and welfare centres prevails all over East Europe, with the exception of some provisions in the larger Polish towns.

From East Europe to Southern Europe, the picture is much the same, or possibly becomes more disheartening. The Humane Movement in Greece has been estimated as being about one hundred years behind that in Northern Europe. Owing to its poverty and political strife, both the humane movement and the working animal population, particularly in the crushing poverty of remote rural Greece, have fared badly. It is fairly common for horses and donkeys too old to be of any further use, simply to be turned loose in country without any pasture.

Italy and Portugal have no high record for draught-animal welfare, in spite of there being Animal Protection Societies recognized in both countries, particularly the Anglo-Italian Society for the Protection of Horses, which has brought some pressure to bear, as well as innumerable interested foreign tourists and residents. Parts of both countries suffer from poverty and backward methods and attitudes, and some traditional hostility to interference by Welfare Societies.

In the Italian provinces of Umbria and Tuscany, the dairy cow, of the thin Brahmah type is also used for work, which seems an uneconomical and overstraining use of this 'dual-purpose' animal.

In Spain there is still a widespread utilization of horses, mules and donkeys, in spite of increasing mechanisation and prosperity, and the prohibition of horse-drawn traffic from some city centres, such as Madrid.

Probably overloading, especially in view of the mountainous character of much of the country and the long steep gradients to be traversed in often blazing temperatures, combined with poor feeding and inadequate veterinary care, is the worst aspect.

Donkeys are still used in road construction, carrying heavy panniers of stones and sand. During the construction of the United States oil pipeline to feed the American bases built in Spain in the mid to late 1950s the most modern heavy earth-moving machinery was employed by the United States contractors on the project; while the Spanish contractors, Agroman SA, a Jesuit enterprise and one of the largest and most influential in Spain, were using men with picks and shovels — (to aid the unemployment situation)—and donkeys. We frequently saw donkeys brought down and falling over with unduly heavy loads, and lashed to make them struggle to their feet again. Upon investigation, ill-fitting and badly repaired harnesses and worn-out panniers had often caused severe galling and wounding, but still the animals continued working. In frequent cases draught animals are muzzled, which may denote that they have been made vicious by ill-treatment.

From a villa on the summit of the Sierra Morena, overlooking the valley of Cordoba, a long steep ascent of some ten miles or more, we many times witnessed horses and donkeys stumbling, and slipping on their forelegs, because in spite of all their straining, and the whipping of the carters, the carts, usually the oldfashioned heavy wooden type with large wheels, simply could not be got up the hill. Heavy loads of coal from Cordoba were delivered to the villas in the Sierra in this type of cart, pulled by light horse (probably an old riding or carriage horse) and a tiny leader donkey, which struggled up the hills from early morning till late at night. Their carter was, however, a humane man who although asthmatical, carried the coal sacks hundreds of yards on his own shoulders when the horse could go no higher. We pointed out to the owner of the coal firm that it would be more economical, as well as more humane, to have a lorry and get more deliveries done. He insisted that the animals were 'cheaper'. Such a horse, when finally too old and infirm to be of any further use whatever in a cart, will probably be contracted for the bull-ring and fetch a few pounds for its final agonies, until it is too injured to stagger any more into the arena. The attitude of the coal merchant shows that it is not poverty alone which is at the root of much of this problem in countries where there is little awakened social conscience with regard to animal suffering.

Long-distance donkeys and mules in 'trains' in particular suffer from galls and foot and tendon troubles. Often they had been indiscriminately 'fired' by some horse coper and not given enough time for rest and recovery. Loads could often have been more intelligently distributed, although some muleteers were co-operative when spoken to.

In general it is very difficult to get any measures taken, or public resentment aroused, even at acts of deliberate cruelty, such as a case we witnessed in Valencia where a cart-horse had sores like ribbons of raw flesh under the harness and was working in a cart hauling heavy stones, or another in Cadiz where a youth had a cart with a donkey and habitually rained blows on its head for no apparent reason until blood actually flowed. In neither case when we remonstrated, were we supported by the onlookers or the authorities.

Between two or three thousand horses, mules and donkeys are cared for every year in Spain by the International League for the Protection of Horses, and receive medical and surgical treatment, but this is just scratching the surface. Prior to the Civil war, there was some officially organized animal welfare, but we believe the present regime and ecclesiastical authorities do not encourage its resurgence, although Spain is now emerging into modernization and prosperity.

A common sight in all the relatively poor and underdeveloped countries is the horse, mule, donkey, camel or even bullock plodding round in endless weary circles at water-mills and tread-mills, and labouring in the scorching fields. The law of Moses made the injunction that the ox and ass should not be yoked together for ploughing and that animals treading corn should be unmuzzled, but it is common to see these basic and common-sense principles disregarded everywhere.

As for the cab-horse, in varying stages of well-groomed dejection to complete skeleton-like decrepitude, it is to be found from Marrakesh to Killarney, from Rome and Pisa to Las Palmas, from Calcutta to Bangalore. Many travellers regard this form of transport as part of the scenery, standing out in all weathers, exploited in relative degrees by avaricious drivers, wringing a meagre living to the utmost that can be extracted during the tourist season. And if this can be true of tourists abroad it is to a lesser extent true nearer home. In the Channel Islands, the Dame of Sark has forbidden motor traffic on her privately owned domain with the result that horses ply between the Harbour and the high plateau, carrying holiday makers. It is a strenuous climb and soft-hearted visitors have been known to walk in order to spare the horses. Heavy luggage is now being taken up the steep hill road by tractor.

Foreign visitors to Egypt have often expressed concern at the state of some of the animals used, mainly by tourists, in the Pyramid and

Sphinx areas of Giza and of the bad driving and riding that is allowed to go on—for which many tourists are quite as much to blame as the owners of the camels, horses and donkeys. The Tourist Board in Cairo has received many complaints about the treatment and condition of these animals. At a meeting held in April 1968 attended by representatives of the Police, the Tourist Police and Tourist Board, comments were invited from representatives of the Brooke Hospital in Cairo. It was suggested that notices should be posted asking the public to report all cruelty or ill-treatment cases to the Police; the Police in their turn to report all complaints to the Tourist Board; that owners and their employees carry their registered numbers in English and Arabic; the Police to forbid the use of all debilitated and lame animals and all reckless and bad driving; the sand-carts to be *walked* up hill and down hill and only trotted on the flat; a simple shelter and water to be provided on the Midan and restaurant side of the Pyramids for the animals (the Brooke Hospital to pay for the erection of a water-trough here, if allowed).

In 1969 the numbers of animals in the Pyramid area, registered for riding and for carts, were three hundred camels, two hundred horses and fifty donkeys. Mr Adel Tahir, Under Secretary of State for Tourism, said he did not want the Police to have to interfere with the owners and their boys, but the bad impression made on the tourist by their treatment of the animals would have to cease. The animals should be used in rotation; overloading of the sand-carts with galloping up and down hill was needless cruelty; the boy employees should also be licensed and not allowed to try and force the animals to do tricks, such as dancing, to amuse the tourists, and the Veterinary Department would be asked to send an inspector on surprise checks.

Some moves are also afoot in Luxor to provide revolutionary amelioration for the working animals, by erecting a drinking-trough at Luxor Railway Station—also to be donated by the Brooke Hospital—to prevent overloading of the gharries by restricting the number of passengers carried, to withdraw the worst of the gharry horses by degrees for humane destruction, to withdraw licences from bad owners for overloading, driving their animals when lame, galloping, beating and whipping them, and underfeeding, and to begin to reduce the number of licences issued yearly, to erect simple shelters with water for the donkeys on the west bank used by the tourists. These suggestions are excellent where, when and if implemented.

The Brooke Hospital for Animals in Cairo has evolved from the Old War Horse Memorial Hospital which in turn grew out of the Old War

Horse Rescue Campaign in progress from 1930 to 1934. It was about 1930 that Major General Geoffrey Brooke's wife noticed that many of the horses and mules hauling the overloaded carts and carriages in Cairo were branded with the mark of the British Army on their flanks.

Her enquiries and investigations revealed that at the end of the 1918 war, the horses and mules of the Army had been sold to local owners, as there was then an acute shipping shortage and it was impossible to bring them all home again. Appeals in the British Press brought Mrs Brooke funds with which to start buying up the old war horses, from heart-breaking conditions. It was thought that not more than a few hundred at most could have survived the appalling conditions in which they were toiling, described by Mrs Brooke as bitter servitude. But the number rescued was around the five thousand mark.

This campaign of rescue lasted for four years. In 1934 the hospital was opened. Mrs Brooke seeing the pitiful plight of the native working animals, realized that the only answer was 'a free veterinary hospital, where the horses, donkeys and mules would be treated, and their very poor owners given instruction in the care of their beasts. Funds were still to hand from the flood of donations sent in at the time of the Old War Horse Rescue Campaign, with which Mrs Brooke was able to open her hospital in Cairo, and commence her magnificent pioneering work.

The enormous difficulties attendant on a task of this sort in a foreign country can well be envisaged.

Mrs Kathleen Taylor-Smith, Treasurer of the Brooke Hospital, has this to say:

> ...there are still many things we would like to see improved [in England]. But those who love animals must often wonder how they fare in the countries which have few laws passed to protect them, no free clinics where poor people can obtain veterinary help and advice for their working animals and where public opinion is not roused at the sight of cruelty.

As an article from the *Arab Observer* of December 1963, reprinted by kind permission of the Editor of the Middle East News Agency, points out:

> Men sometimes work their animals when they are clearly unfit to pull a load, not from intentional cruelty but out of necessity, which can also prevent the animal from being properly fed...Today harness wounds and galls have decreased considerably, but increased motor traffic constitutes a far worse danger for draught animals and many accidents occur.

There are some sixty thousand carts drawn by horse, mule or donkey working in and around Cairo at the present time, and innumerable pack animals, who are constantly endangered by the carelessly driven vehicles and may be seriously injured by their own loads. In particular lime or acid carelessly loaded can be very dangerous and in case of stumbling or accident the animal suffers intensive and extensive burns. Those animals who come to the Hospital too worn out and unfit for further work are painlessly put to sleep and their owners receive compensation towards the cost of buying a new animal—also paid by the Hospital Funds.

The Brooke Hospital has had five water troughs erected in the country markets near Cairo, and there is one more outside the Hospital. Animals haul carts twenty miles or more to the markets and then stay all day long under the burning sun and choking dust, without finding any water to allay their terrible thirst, and then either go on the long weary, thirsty trek home again, or even on to yet another market.

Observers report that in the summer the queue for the Hospital trough stretches right down the road, and some poor animals are so frantic with thirst that the men have a struggle to control them in their carts. It is estimated that at least two hundred each day stop to drink at the trough.

In connection with all the rebuilding in progress in Cairo, it has been noted by onlookers that the state of the working animals cannot be said to have improved lately. The shortage of vans, trucks and cars of all sorts, means that very heavy loads of building materials etc. are put into carts pulled by animals totally unfit for such work. Dr Murad (the veterinary surgeon) spotted one such grossly overloaded cart near the hospital and when he insisted on having some of the contents removed and left by the roadside for a second journey, the poor horse went on its way with a better hope of reaching its destination. It was actually being expected to pull three tons of cement in bags of about one hundredweight, an impossibility as soon as it was faced with the slightest incline, of course. As so much new building is going up all over the country, it is not to be wondered that strains, lameness, spinal injuries and accidents take such a heavy toll of these poor creatures... Mechanization is slow to spread to the country districts and the poorest people will rely for many years yet on their beasts of burden for their own livelihood. More and more horse traffic is being banned from the centre of towns—and rightly so for the fast motor traffic is murder to small donkeys, mules and horses in the carts but the animals are working on just the same wherever they are and *have the same conditions, in the majority of cases* as when Mrs Brooke shouldered her great task in rescuing the old war horses after the First World War.

The Hospital vets buy on an average some four hundred and fifty horses, mules and donkeys a year for humane destruction, 'the majority in outlying markets from the poorest and most ignorant of men. In mechanized western countries it is impossible to imagine the toil and suffering endured by these little derelicts.

From over a thousand animals treated in the Hospital annually, and about seven thousand in the surrounding markets, the highest percentage is due to sores and accident, than to debility and lameness. Most cases of lameness and emaciation result from overloading the animals and forcing them to continuous work, even in the heat of the day, without giving them the required rest, all exacerbated by the high cost of forage which prevents the poverty-stricken owners from feeding their animals adequately. And so is set up the chain reaction of stumbling from weariness, injury, beating, and perhaps firing by some backstreet farrier, for totally unrelated ills, which, with working before proper recovery, brings down the animal's condition to an even lower level.

In 1967, the 8th May edition of the leading Egyptian newspaper *Al Ahram* reported the following:

> The Minister of Agriculture, Dr Shafiq el Khishin has decided to take severe measures against anyone who uses cruelty against animals and birds etc., on the following lines, exhausting horses or donkeys by making them carry more than their age or strength justifies; the use of any animal which is injured or paralysed:...

But we have seen the seemingly insuperable barriers existing against the implementation of such humane intentions. Carts continue to be grossly overloaded, draught animals continue to work on, injured, galled, underfed; and goaded camels, bewildered and frightened among the traffic and noise of the city, having made the incredible journey on foot from Libya and the Sudan, continue to be mercilessly beaten from the streets and end in the markets exhausted and starved until they are sold off for food.

The conditions and problems are the same all over North Africa.

In the winter of 1921 two British ladies, Mrs Frances Hosali and her daughter set off for a six months' holiday in North Africa, in search of sunshine. As reported by Colin Jackson in a broadcast BBC talk on 25 January, 1955

> But, as it was that light-hearted journey changed their whole lives...
> They went into the Arab market places and around the alleys and

small out-of-the-way villages...And what they found on their journey horrified them. Mrs Hosali, who had always been fond of animals, saw cases of the most dreadful cruelty...She found pack animals being goaded and beaten; she found horses hopping crippled on three legs... donkeys being tortured by drunken masters...Their sunshine holiday became a nightmare pilgrimage.

Back in Britain, Mrs Hosali kept thinking of the horrible sights she had seen, the sufferings of so many helpless animals...And so, in 1923 starting quite alone, she founded the Society for the Protection of Animals in North Africa...She decided to give up everything in England, and leaving her family home and friends behind her, she went herself...The French authorities said she was wasting her time... that going out alone into places seldom visited by Europeans was dangerous.

To start off from chosen centres she visited Arab market towns nearby. She went into the fondouks—the local stable yards. In these places tethered up, there would be usually fifty or a hundred donkeys and mules. And Mrs Hosali used to take off the pack saddles of the animals and treated their sores and wounds herself. Astonished Arabs would crowd round both bewildered and fascinated but also keen to learn how to treat the animals sores...As the months went by Mrs Hosali trained Arab dressers to help her and they too went out to the markets to treat the thousands of suffering animals.

And the Society is still doing so today, as well as running permanent hospitals and clinics. However, the territory covered by this gallant and courageous pioneering society is enormous, comprising Libya, Tunisia, Algeria and Morocco—mountainous terrain, widely scattered and backward communities. It is something like the distance from Lisbon to Moscow, so one can only lament how thinly-spread is this humane work for which there is such desperate need.

Clive Aspinall, the former Organizing Secretary of SPANA, was concerned that the uneasy aftermath of the Arab-Israeli War, hit all North Africa financially:

When people suffer financially, their animals suffer...The price of all food stuffs goes up and the working horses, mules and donkeys get even less feed of all sorts. This is followed by a marked decrease in the stamina and resistance of working animals to injury and disease. They tire quicker and work harder, and when a horse is undernourished and weary, he does not pick up his feet, and stumbles or falls and if between shafts, a shaft often breaks causing serious injuries while, in any case, the horse often breaks his knees. As for the owner himself, tired and harassed by money problems, he quickly loses his patience and sense of proportion, and is often not slow with his whip or stick to take out on his unfortunate animal his own frustrations! Thus, the ugly trail of cause and effect drags on...and as human worry and suffering increases so it is passed on and handed down to the animals and in doing so, is increased tenfold.

On the outskirts of the labyrinth of crowded alleyways which form the Souk, or Arab bazaar, are the wholesale markets. 'Standing around the wholesale markets we find ranks of low, flat carts with their horses, mules and drivers, waiting to take away the bulk purchases from these markets to shops, restaurants, hotels etc. These animals are usually owned by very poor men, who hire themselves and their animals out by the hour. Their fees are extremely low, as one driver competes vociferously against his neighbour for employment, and in consequence, the unfortunate animals are always in wretched condition, while carts and harness reflect the poverty of both driver and animal. The wheels of carts appear about to disintegrate, whilst the harness is an indiscriminate, hotch-potch of cracked old leather, frequently mended with wire and held together with lengths of rope or rusty chain and twisted, broken buckles. The terrible North African ring bit usually adds its own particular torture to the ensemble.

Major Aspinall continues:

> For a people who are so utterly dependent on horses, donkeys and mules, for all forms of their transport, it is almost incomprehensible how atrociously ignorant the ordinary North African remains of the most rudimentary principles of caring for their animals. The tragedy is that this ignorance, almost invariably goes hand-in-hand with complete callousness of the intense suffering which this ignorance causes.

The Arab farrier charges four shillings and sixpence for shoeing all round and completes his job in about nineteen minutes. SPANA are endeavouring to train them in correct methods of farriery, but it is slow uphill work. They are now campaigning for the abolition of the 'diabolical bits' which are everywhere found in the countries of North Africa. Horses and donkeys and mules are daily brought into the hospitals and clinics suffering from the most appalling injuries to mouth, tongue and jaws caused solely by the use of native bits. These instruments of torture, for such they are, are quite terrible when brand new, but when they are old and worn, and 'repaired' with wire, they become the very instruments of the devil.

These bits exercise such agonizingly drastic control necessary for the spectacular ceremonial charges at full gallop, and rearing to a sudden stop, when accompanied by yelling and firing and rearing back on hind legs to an instantaneous halt. The horses' tongues are not infrequently severed right across or appallingly injured by this bit. The most common is the ring bit which is placed into the mouth, with the forward part of the bit resting on the 'bars' — the space behind the incisor teeth—and across the inside of the mouth. The 'tongue' of the bit, to which the reins are attached supply the leverage. The sharp upper edge of the 'tongue' very soon produces an open sore in the chin groove, which gets progressively worse.

Then there is the traditional iron bit, with a barbarous deep and heavy mouth piece, which stands up in a sharp high rectangle from the bit bar and presses right into the roof of the mouth. When one of these was taken from the mouth of a mule standing in a Marrakesh Fondouk, one of the rope-reins (cut when the bit was removed) was fastened to a loop of wire through which the mule's tongue passed! The other rein was tied to one of the 'cannons' of the bit. The tongue and corners of the mule's mouth were found to be badly injured. The bars of the mouth were red-raw. The animal was standing harnessed to his cart, his head low to the ground, and a steady stream of blood and saliva drooled from his bleeding lips. On being approached he squealed and nearly kicked the bottom out of his cart, but on having the bit removed his whole attitude changed to quietness and complete amenability. Yet animals such as these, suffering and abused in this way, are often the sole bread-winners of these poor families, who, without their animal, would literally starve.

The drivers, carters and other owners, who receive the new humane English bits, find that they have a fitter animal than when the Arab bit was used, that it pulls or carries his load with greater ease and cheerfulness, is able to work longer and still, at the end of a hard day, appears to be fresher than formerly. SPANA is also seeing whether the issue of plastic hose, to cover the cutting ropes used to keep the *burdah* in place which give rise to so many galls and wounds, will prove practical, and as beneficial as the replacement, where possible, of the barbarous native bits. Often worn saddle bags, combined with gross overloading, cause eighty per cent of back wounds and the typical cases of terribly infected hips. During the long days at the *souk*, the heavy saddles and galling saddle bags are never removed at all, to give the animal even an hour of relief. Possibly the animals will have already plodded ten or even twenty miles with their loads and carts to the *souk*, passengers often riding two up on some debilitated animal. On arrival the animal will be tied up and left. Some three thousand animals will have made this weary journey. They are left, as a matter of common practice, without food or water and the agonizing bit is not even removed. The SPANA dressers work steadily along the line, treating up to six hundred animals at a *souk* in a day. When the great saddles are taken off, often quite unbelievably sore backs, girth galls, trace galls and crupper galls are revealed. The lesser cases are treated on the spot; the extreme cases are taken away to hospital.

In the evening the families and groups of friends reassemble near their transport. Throughout the day, whether it has been hot or cold, wet or dry, no one amongst the perhaps five thousand people who have attended the *souk* have given a thought to their transport, any more than they would have given a thought to the municipal bus, had there been one!

And so begins the long painful trek home again. In the town *fondouks*, or stable yards, the animals are either tied up or let loose, after being ridden or driven in from the country.

Frequently the *fondouks* are filthy and unprotected from the weather. All animals are coralled indiscriminately together—horses, mules, donkeys, goats, camels and cattle; consequently on a crowded day, and particularly on Friday when the Arabs go to the Mosques, the animals are packed in like sardines. A kicking mule or dangerous bull sets all the animals off, so that the smaller donkeys get a very bad time indeed and results can be serious, with terrible injuries inflicted.

In the countries of Latin and Central America, pack and draught animals are still extensively used, and include lumber and ranch horses, and have to work in the same conditions which spell suffering and hardship for them everywhere; ignorance, poverty, callousness, lack of medicines and veterinary care, the prevalence of primitive superstitions and inherited attitudes, plus hazards from careless mechanization. Additionally, there are extremes of temperature and altitude and social conditions seldom stable enough to enforce animal welfare laws. Many of the Latin-American countries view suffering with fatality and indifference; in some, bull-fighting and cock-fighting are legal, methods of destruction of stray animals primitive and heartless, humane slaughter unknown and transportation is often bad in the extreme, so it is not surprising that the gross abuse of the working animal is regarded with scant attention. Here and there more enlightened enclaves exist, but even then, either organization, funds, personnel, will or political stability are lacking to concretize them; and generally speaking, it may be said that South and Central America is covered with dark expanses of animal abuse and suffering.

However, it is not necessary only to go to underdeveloped countries, with a long history of poverty and ignorance, to find the working horse, man's first 'servant', being callously abused. In the New Brunswick SPCA news of 1966 it was reported that although the horse has disappeared from their streets, he has not disappeared from the Province 'He survives as a beast of burden, in our forest industry, often neglected sometimes cruelly abused, and almost always hidden from sight'. It is only occasionally, through press, television or radio that the public are made aware of terrible acts of cruelty to horses that have worked long and hard in the woods of Eastern Canada. But although there was a public outcry for it, constant inspection is difficult and very costly.

Anyone who is acquainted with the lumber industry, knows the rough, dangerous conditions under which the horse hauling timber must work. Those of us who can recall horse-drawn timber carriages in Britain earlier this century (in some areas they were used well into the 1930s) will know that the work involves some of the heaviest, hardest labour any horse is called upon to perform and against which ploughing is comparatively light work, although the plough horse's day finished in the early afternoon. Often merciless flogging was needed to get the timber moving from a dead weight start, particularly in heavy woodland conditions where the rides could be axle deep in loam. When cornering, all the strain would be on the animal actually in the shafts, the trace horses could exert little help or the load would be pulled askew. Young, or unfit horses or any not up to their work could be literally pulled off their feet by the rest of the team. Those who did not pull their weight often through no fault of their own, would feel the stockwhip without mercy. These hardships translated to the Canadian backwoods with perhaps bad stabling conditions and perfunctory attention to welfare can be on a par with the gun-carriage horses of the 1914 war. Those that survived were permanently flat-footed and with deformed gait from pulling impossibly heavy loads under the worst possible conditions. It is estimated that as many as 45,000 horses are used in the forestry industry of New Brunswick, and some thousand horses leave the Province destined for the slaughter houses of Quebec, where they are joined by four thousand from Ontario, four thousand from Quebec and one thousand or so from other parts of Canada.

Mr Brian Davies, Executive Secretary for the New Brunswick SPCA says that most of the people involved in the forest products industry of New Brunswick are of British or French descent.

The horses are used in lieu of mechanical equipment where the ground is rough or the operator short of money, both reasons which lead to abuse of the animals involved. The mechanization of the industry is proceeding fairly rapidly so that the numbers of horses labouring in the woods is decreasing, although it seems likely there will always be a significant number of horses working. Another contributing factor to the problem is that today few people know how to care for horses properly, and tend to treat them like automobiles. This particular facet of the problem will, undoubtedly, get even worse.

The lumber teams are not the only Canadian work horses to give rise to disquiet among humanely-minded people. A. G. Street, the well known farmer, writer and broadcaster, who was in Canada after the First World War, remarked on the farming practice there of turning out work horses to fend for themselves during the Canadian winter. He admitted a few did not survive the rigours of low temperature and heavy snowfalls, but those that did seemed none the worse for the experience and it was found to be sound economic practice to leave these animals to fend for themselves. It would seem to be the old survival of the fittest laws of nature at work again.

This happens in the British Isles also though our snow drifts do not often reach the extremes of a Canadian winter. Dartmoor particularly reveals many carcasses or emaciated survivors after each hard winter. Horse dealers seem to share the same outlook over the exploitation of their horseflesh. It is an attitude which persists all over the globe wherever there are draught animals.

# *Blinded by Science*

'There is something dreadful, satanic in tormenting those who have never harmed us, who cannot defend themselves and who are utterly in our power.
CARDINAL NEWMAN

*The Times* of 20 December 1967 contained a lengthy feature on the behaviour of newts. We quote:

> Newts were blinded by cutting out their eyes and were made to walk along a straight two hundred yard course before being transferred to the test arena. Afterwards, and most surprisingly, most of the newts moved in the opposite direction, like the normally sighted newts in earlier experiments. Further tests showed that the blinded newts, like sighted newts, are disorientated on cloudy days when the sun is not visible.

A detailed account of these experiments ended with:

> It seems certain that newts are guided towards their home waters by a compass mechanism dependent on the sun and not on their sense of smell.

These experiments appeared to pass without any official comment. There was however one comment in the correspondence columns of *The Times* from a lady living in Norfolk, who wrote:

> I read in The Times Science Report that at Mississippi State University newts were blinded by cutting out their eyes so that their orientation by the sun could be observed when they were sightless. Apparently both sighted and sightless newts are guided by the sun and confused on cloudy days. Is this discovery of sufficient importance to justify cutting out the eyes of living and suffering creatures?

It is a pertinent question that could be asked of a great deal of scientific experiment on living creatures. The first dog in space brought an outcry by dog-lovers from Russia to America.

We saw the space capsule in which Laika, the first 'canine hero' of the USSR, took that epoch-making flight. It fitted the dog almost as a skin fits a sausage, there was no room for it to move or to get to its feet, and it could only lie in one position for the entire flight. The capsule is on view at the Exhibition of Soviet Economic Achievement in Moscow and, in addition, the Space Room at the Pioneer Camp in Yalta has an exhibition of space photographs and of dogs used in rocket experiments. The director told us that many had not lived.

After Laika's capsule had been sent hurtling through space news-paper headlines proclaimed: 'At Last a Beating Heart in Outer Space'. But, only a few months later, live animals in spacecraft had become so commonplace that when a monkey was incinerated in a rocket which came down in the Pacific, the Press reference stressed the delay in the firing schedule rather than the monkey's fate. A line from Reuter's Press Agency stated: 'Goliath had been in the capsule without food or water for more than fifty-three hours. The launching had originally been scheduled for yesterday.'

After the space dogs we have turtles and tortoises in advance of manned flight to the moon. In November 1968 a report came from Moscow that in addition to flies and mealworms the 'Astro ark' contained turtles and higher forms of life in order that the radiation effects on their spleen might be measured.

Monkeys are used increasingly as the nearest substitute for man, not only to test vaccines, nerve gases or new forms of surgery, but to discover reactions to weightlessness inside rockets or injury in crashing motor-cars. In the latter tests pregnant baboons have been used to assess the effects of car seat belts on expectant human mothers who may be involved in head-on car crashes. Yet they are not of human weight or proportions and their arms and legs are formed differently and behave differently under crash conditions.

Monkeys are tested for just about everything from the effects of heavy smoking to exposure to atomic rays after nuclear explosions. They are put in 'Zeigler' chairs to study electric shock treatment, operated upon in order to study the effects of leucotomy, given gastric ulcers, anthrax, malaria, rabies and syphilis. In fact they are 'guinea pigs' for every ill the flesh is heir to, including quite a few that are purposely man-induced. So it is not surprising that the supply of monkeys, or 'subhumans', is dwindling and that scientists are growing anxious and preparing breeding supplies of their own.

On the death of a heart transplant patient, a trustee of a New York hospital and several medical foundations appealed for funds to start a breeding programme to make possible the use of apes in heart transplant research. *The Times* correspondent from New York commented:

> The bulk of heart transplant research has been on dogs, partly because apes are expensive and partly because there are not enough of them. Indeed there have been several alarms over the years about the danger to the primate populations of south east Asia and the Amazon where a steady trade in apes and monkeys has reduced numbers in areas where the factors which determine the natural balance of nature and consequent survival of the species, are imperfectly known. This is particularly true of the South American jungle, where recent ecological research, has suggested that, in spite of the abundance of warmth, water and undergrowth, survival of animals is a much less simple and more localized matter than had been supposed.

The boom in heart transplant experiments has resulted in an increased demand for the primates, particularly baboons. British airports handle 25,000 'subhumans' a year, American airports about 60,000, and this does not take into account the demands of Continental laboratories or of Pharmacia, Uppsala, the huge Swedish concern, or the vast programmes of the USSR in every field of scientific experiment.

Group-Captain Douglas Bader, crippled hero of the Second World War, writes:

> In this day and age it is hideous to contemplate the sufferings of these animals captured in a hot country; crammed together with barely adequate food and water; put into an aeroplane and flown thousands of miles, terrified by the noise and unaccustomed feeling of being in the air; being landed in winter at the cold airports of Europe and America. And then many lose their short lives in experiments by scientists. It is a shameful reflection on our human standards that this can be allowed to continue.
>
> Scientists say they use animals in search of knowledge to benefit the human race. But the word science covers a wide field—from experiments on animals to nuclear weapons. Knowledge can be used for good or evil and the record shows that science has no moral code. It is time this sacred word was put in its proper perspective. Being a so-called scientist does not exempt a man from the normal moral obligations of a civilized human being. Kindness to animals should form part of such a code.

Soon after Group-Captain Bader had made this protest there was another 'incident' of monkeys dying in transit before ever they reached the experimental laboratories. We quote from an RSPCA report:

> Considerable press publicity was given on October 7th to another monkey tragedy. This concerned a cargo of three hundred and ninety-five monkeys and baboons sent by air from Nairobi of which on arrival

at London Airport, one hundred and five were found to be dead. Post mortems showed that some of them died of suffocation, and it was stated that they were grossly overcrowded. Forty-two baboons were dead out of a total of fifty-eight crammed into six boxes, each of which measured only three feet eleven inches by one foot four inches by three feet. One wonders how they could have packed into such a space. Most, if not all, of these animals were destined to be used in laboratories.

After all the previous horrors of this kind that have occurred in recent years it seems incredible that such gross overcrowding should still occur. It was stated in the reports that the plane was delayed by a mechanical fault at Khartoum and was grounded for a period of sixteen hours in very high temperature; but this is no excuse at all for the tight packing and the neglect which led to such suffering and loss of life.

The forests of the world are being stripped of primates at the rate of not less than 200,000 a year, often by cruel and wasteful methods, and the demand is ever increasing. Many die soon after capture, many more in transit. In 1954 there were so many casualties at London Airport and the outcry by the general public after press coverage was so vehement that the Government of India put a temporary ban on the export of monkeys. But handsome profits had been made which dealers would not easily forgo, and the ban was rapidly withdrawn and replaced by an undertaking that monkeys would only be consigned to 'such parties abroad as have been certified by the Government of the country concerned as being "genuinely involved in medical research or the production of medical preparations".'

In 1967 it looked as if the subhumans might have their revenge. Longtailed green or Vervet monkeys from Uganda, imported into West Germany, brought with them a curious liver disease which research workers contracted. In spite of strict quarantine restrictions, eight people died of this disease and many more were extremely ill. No special import licence was required for the traffic in these monkeys and no veterinary examination was made after their arrival in Germany. The World Health Organization called for the suspension of imports of Vervet monkeys and the anti-vivisection societies pointed out the dangers of using subhumans for experiments to control disease in humans. They pointed afresh to the thalidomide tragedy, which the vivisectors said was due to insufficient experiment and testing while the anti-vivisection lobby suggested it was the result of assuming that effects on human beings would be the same as effects on animals.

Thalidomide was clinically tested on animals for six years in the German laboratories where it was first manufactured; on rats for toxicity, on cats for blood-pressure, on rabbits for fever and on guinea

148

pigs for allergy, but it was not thought necessary to test effects on foetuses.

In the USA, which did not market Thalidomide, Eleanor Seiling, President of United Action for Animals, called for safer drugs in a pamphlet beginning: 'The present methods of drug-testing, which are archaic, unscientific and cruel, do not produce safe drugs'.

The American Medical Association admitted that 'drug activity in animals is no assurance of similar activity in humans, and for some human disorders there is no similar disorder in animals...Frequently animal studies prove little or nothing and are very difficult or impossible to correlate to humans.'

Yet the experiments continue to proliferate. In Britain alone in the year 1968 there were something approaching five million experiments, 87 per cent without anaesthetic, carried out in six hundred laboratories (some of them covering many acres of ground). Under the 1876 Cruelty to Animals Act, certain safeguards for laboratory animals were laid down, but with so many loopholes that not one prosecution for cruelty has been brought by the Home Office under this Act. No one would suppose it is because experiment *never* involves any suffering. Until recently there were three Government Inspectors to visit and 'sign the book' of British laboratories. This has now been increased to eight. The scope and complexity of laboratory work involving live animals could hardly have been envisaged in 1876. Who, for instance, in those closing years of the nineteenth century could have envisaged the work of the microbiological warfare laboratories at Porton on Salisbury Plain? Kept secret for many years, the work of this establishment became news after a television programme in 1968 entitled *A Plague on Your Children*.

In this programme, Porton was repeatedly referred to, even by American military authorities, but the illustrations on the theme of biological warfare came from Scandinavian laboratories, as filming was not permitted at Porton.

Our attention was first drawn to the work done at this military establishment almost twenty years ago by the consignments of small animals on Waterloo Station labelled for Porton Halt. Having lived for several years only a few miles away from Salisbury, we still had many friends in the area and found that locally this Ministry of Defence project was known as 'The Poison Factory'. It was surrounded by more security than any similar defence installation on Salisbury Plain. The firing ranges, with their possibility of unexploded bombs and their 'Keep Out' notices, were an open playground compared with this

Porton area, where the strong fencing and the warnings about guard dogs and radar screens suggested that something quite unusual was going on inside this forbidden territory.

Some inkling of the activities taking place was gleaned when a local electrician working on maintenance saw something that he was not supposed to see and recounted his experiences to one of the humane societies. His testimony has not been either contradicted or confirmed. A summary of it reads:

> I went a little nearer and looked. It was a small monkey enclosed in a glass case, its eyes seemed to be falling out and it could not breathe. It was in dreadful distress. When I went near it buried its head in its arms and sobbed like a child. The next day I went back and it was nearly finished by then. It had sunk to a little heap at the bottom of the glass case.

This was probably a poison gas experiment. *A Plague on Your Children* referred to mustard gas, manufactured at Porton and allegedly used by Egyptian forces in the Yemen; BZ 'nerve gas' tested on United States soldiers to the point where it deranged but did not entirely wreck their nervous systems (the results being something akin to an overdose of drugs or alcohol); and VX gas, which penetrates skin, bloodstream and lungs. This last gas, a form of 'riot' gas, if used in sufficient quantities in an enclosed space (such as a bunker) can cause death, and has done so in Vietnam.

The television programme also gave the figures of animals used in chemical and biological warfare experiments as 84,000 per year. We were shown some animals entering Porton but were told that none came out. We were also shown a rabbit injected with anthrax and told that it took up to eighteen or twenty-four hours to die. The television cameras were not allowed into Allington Farm, that part of Porton's seven thousand acres devoted to the breeding and maintenance of the experimental animals. We were, however, shown distant views of Gruinard Island off the west coast of Scotland which had been infected with anthrax and was now contaminated and would not support life again for at least a century. The animals killed on the island in the course of this 'experiment' included sheep and deer as well as smaller creatures. In January 1969 it was reported from Washington that Baker Island, a small US possession in the Pacific, 1,700 miles west of Honolulu, was being used as a testing ground for microbiological warfare under cover of a bird study programme.

But it was sheep that first drew attention to the work of the micro-biological scientists, and to Porton in particular, by headlines in the world press on the mysterious death of 6,400 sheep in Skull Valley, Utah, twenty-seven miles away from a US Army nerve gas testing centre at Dugway. At first there was considerable mystery, as more and more sheep took sick and died in a remote area where no possible cause could be found. The military authorities at Dugway must have had their suspicions, because Brigadier General William Stone, director of research and laboratories, stated that healthy sheep given feeds of hay contaminated with nerve gas (i.e. VX) began to show similar symptoms to the casualties in Skull Valley. Headlines on this issue began with phrases like 'Sheep Riddle Persists' and progressed to 'Nerve Gas Threat to US City'.

Under this last headline from *The Times*' correspondent in New York on 20 August 1967 came the news that the United States Defence Department was investigating the danger to people living in the Colorado and Denver areas in the event of a leak in gas storage tanks. It was frighteningly estimated that a mere three per cent of the amount stored would be sufficient to kill off the entire world population 'VX., a persistent agent that remains lethal for days after dispersal, affects the central nervous system and causes convulsions and death from asphyxiation. The report was based upon Army Chemical Corps tests which resulted in the death of six thousand sheep, some of the animals being as much as *45 miles* away from the point where the test gas was released'.

It was later revealed that this gas was perfected and manufactured at Porton.

Mr Seymour M. Hersh, Press Secretary to Senator Eugene Mc-Carthy, in an interview with *The Times* in November 1968, stated that

> The People at Porton Down have superior intellectual and scientific ability and have been guiding America in biological warfare for years... Thus weaponry which America has developed and in many cases is stockpiling, includes frightful nerve Gases—code named GAGB GD VE and VX which cause convulsions and asphyxiation and can be fatal within minutes: and anthrax, encephalomyelitis, plague and tularemia, the psychochemical BZ and nonlethal riot control agents used in Vietnam.

All these agents were first tested out on animals, from anthrax to the arsenical-based riot gases once deemed too dangerous for use against human beings but now employed in riot control by US police forces. They have recently caused serious injury and blindness.

In 1968 the Home Office published its annual report on experiments involving animals in Great Britain. The figures were 4,196,566, or

154,000 more than the preceding year. They include 13,517 experiments on cats, 10,769 on dogs, and 149 on 'members of the horse family'. Some 771,553 experiments were carried out on behalf of Government departments.

After the publication of these figures a few letters appeared in the press, and anxiety was expressed by a number of humane organizations regarding this colossal increase in animal suffering. The official reply was that 'those engaged in experimental work were entitled to do so in reasonable privacy and without undue disturbance'. Answering questions on experiments on living animals, Mr Fletcher Cooke, Under Secretary to the Home Office, said he was well aware of public anxiety:

> But I really can assure you that it is based on a misconception that these experiments, of which there have been a great growth, are in any way *surgical* experiments. The growth is almost entirely due to the fact that now by statute we are required to see that many new substances that are necessary to the health of the human race are injected or fed into animals. In the vast proportion of the cases there is no question of cutting or vivisection in the old sense of the word.

Of course, the Porton monkey and the Utah sheep were not vivisected, or cut up alive. They were poisoned and asphyxiated. Many of these British experiments, like those in America and elsewhere, are concerned with the injection of disease, with the reaction to burning, scalding, electric shock, interference with natural functions, or the results of dietary deficiency.

In Great Britain, after an outcry against pet stealing for hospitals and laboratories, it was announced that special breeding farms would be established for supplying animals for vivisection and experiment. In the United States where no such safeguards for stolen pets apply and no questions are asked when strays from the dog pound end up on the operating table, the Government still voted to spend £300,000 on breeding 'the perfect dog for vivisection'.

The dog must be the right size for heart transplants and without vocal chords, so that it cannot cry out and distress its vivisectors. It is hoped to produce the ideal specimen for such work within five years. The scientists suggest that Labradors are the best for skin-grafting and heart transplant operations, and African Basenjis are good because they cannot bark and so obviate the cutting of vocal chords. Their ideal specimen needs strength, endurance, intelligence and trainability, and, if possible, a warm and gentle disposition.

*A Plague on Your Children* showed just such a dog, soft-eyed and tail-wagging, a beagle-type in appearance, licking the hand that injected it with atropine. As experiments involving pain or distress to animals are not allowed to be filmed in Britain, this particular sequence was taken in Sweden. We were later shown this dog going literally 'up the wall' and issuing pitiful noises, but were assured that later an antidote would be administered. This means that the same dog is used more than once for such experiments, and laboratory assistants in the United States have testified that one dog may be injected with a variety of ailments and be subjected to many kinds of operation and experiments before finally relinquishing its hold on life.

At present there are about twenty companies operating in the United Kingdom which breed animals for experimental purposes. A further animal breeding centre is planned for a disused airfield at Manston in Kent, and as there is much profit and no very heavy overheads involved in encouraging small mammals to multiply, no doubt many other concerns will spring up to feed a growing market.

This will at least eliminate some cruelty to pet owners who, after recent cases in the press, must suffer considerably when their cats and dogs disappear, wondering what the end of them may be. One cat dealer who roamed the streets of a Midland town with cat-catching equipment stated that he earned £50 a week from selling his catches to laboratories and universities, and hoped to step it up to £100 per week. Not all of these cats were unwanted strays, and although people have long been warned about turning out their cats at night, some cats feel the call of a 'night on the tiles' so strongly that it is well-nigh impossible to keep them indoors.

The Scottish author Alasdair Alpin MacGregor has described how he visited a laboratory and found 'twenty-seven cats in varying stages of slow dying in a vivisector's laboratory attached to a London hospital. The experiments were performed to see how long the animals could live without parts of their anatomy. This cat died in convulsions in my arms seventeen days after legal professional mutilation. It had a wound a foot in length.'

Pet owners' fears that if their animals fall into dealers' hands they will suffer are not without foundation.

An American laboratory assistant, who took the job because she 'loved animals and wanted to work with them' has described in a *Reader's Digest* article how her charges suffered—not merely from the actual experiment made upon them, but from the conditions under which they were kept: slatted floors so that their claws grew out and curled under, complete lack of exercise, and much callousness on the part of their keepers who saw so much pain and suffering that inevitably they became hardened to their charges' distress when they regained consciousness after surgery.

The American girl's evidence was echoed by a porter at a large teaching hospital in London who testified:

> I worked there for three years and saw hundreds of dogs come in and their cut-up bodies burned in the incinerator. Sometimes they were greyhounds too old to race, or just not fast enough to win races. The worst was at night when a stitched-up dog would come round and begin to moan and scream with pain.
>
> There was one mongrel bitch with her head stitched who kept trying to struggle to her feet and get out of her cage. Next day the man who delivered the dogs told me that she had only had pups the day before. His van delivered dogs two or three times a week, usually very early in the morning while the city was asleep.

Dogs, unless they have had their vocal chords cut, suffer noisily, but monkeys, the nearest to man himself, probably endure even more. Consider Dr Pinneo's monkeys, a report of which was published in *Nature* in January 1966. The Science correspondent of the *Observer* hears echoes of Orwell's *1984* in the following:

> Dr Pinneo has now identified precise points in primitive parts of the brain, each of which seem to correspond to a particular relatively simple movement, such as extending a limb, curling a tail, opening and closing the mouth. Sites controlling rate of heartbeat and breathing were also found.
>
> After locating a series of sites Dr Pinneo implanted up to six probes in the brains of three monkeys. After the animals had recovered from the operation, electric pulses were sent through the probes in various sequences, building up complex movements of various kinds, some like those seen in nature, others quite abnormal. The stimulus overrode any natural movement which the animal happened to be making at the moment, and worked whether it was awake, asleep or anaesthetized.
>
> When connections between the regions with the probes and higher brain regions were surgically cut, the movements could still be elicited. This, says Dr Lawrence, supports the theory that these lower parts of the nervous system contain a kind of toolbox of built-in 'behaviour fragments', simple movements which the higher brain integrates into more complex behaviour.
>
> The experimental monkeys died from brain inflammation before their marionette behaviour could be filmed. It is hoped to overcome this by using smaller probes, Dr Lawrence says. In due course, he reports, it is hoped to establish groups of monkeys under 'programmed' electrical control, so that the researchers can direct them to perform various kinds of complex social behaviour found in nature.
>
> These techniques, he adds, might also in due course be tried on

human beings paralysed by strokes or Parkinson's disease. Deliberate electrical stimulation of appropriate points in the lower brain might elicit movements of the limbs which the damaged part of the higher brain can no longer direct.

The following week an uneasy reader commented on the report:

> Sir, As your Science Correspondent suggests, there is indeed a 1984-ish prospect of Dr Pinneo's experiments in America on the control of monkeys by brain-implanted electrodes. There is more than a whiff of Auschwitz, too.
>
> Those who feel uneasy at such reports would like to know on whose authority such experiments could be made in this country. At present one is tempted to think that the morality behind some usages of animals is no greater than 'if I want to do it, it's all right.'

The Editor of the *Observer* considered this reader's comment sufficiently important to forward it to the director of the Universities Federation for Animal Welfare, who replied:

> We have shown this letter to Mr Walter Scott, Scientific Director of the Universities Federation for Animal Welfare (UFAW). He writes 'I have consulted one of my colleagues who works with monkeys and we are both firmly of the opinion that the experiments carried out by Dr Pinneo would not have been allowed in the UK, except under a special licence from the Home Office. To obtain such a licence, which is quite specific to the particular experiment involved, the licensee must satisfy the authorities that the proposed procedures are essential for the advancement of knowledge, and also that the results would be vitiated if the animals were anaesthetized. Such licences are only sparingly approved by the Home Office and additional conditions relevant to the Pain Rule are often imposed.
>
> I would very much doubt if the experiments carried out by Dr Pinneo really contributed much to the advancement of knowledge, and certainly his techniques, which resulted in monkeys dying from "brain inflammation before their marionette behaviour could be filmed" are quite deplorable, both scientifically and aesthetically'.

The law forbidding the photographing or televising of 'cruel' experiments in Britain has meant that many illustrations of how the human race use animals in the course of research must come from elsewhere. After supplying TV pictures for *A Plague on Your Children*, the great laboratories of Pharmacia, Uppsala, refused us permission to view their 'Animal House' when accompanying a tour of important US doctors and their wives on a visit to the plant.

In *The Animal's Defender* of October 1968 Jane Carding describes visits to laboratories in Greece, USA and Japan, and counteracts the popular belief that 'animals are used for experimental purposes only in gleaming white laboratories by men dedicated to relief of human suffering and inhibited by a dislike of causing pain'.

In Japan she found the experiments were often carried out in unsanitary cellars in order to provide doctors with advanced degrees so that they might open lucrative private practices. 'I have seen men place boxes in which they had crucified rats and opened up their abdomens, placed in cold water so that their nose and mouth remained just above water level, to stay there all night.'

In the USA 'animals were scientifically blinded, deafened and deprived of their sense of smell' and she comments on the duplication of painful experiments because of a rivalry between institutions. In Greece she saw

> small dogs dragged into the operating theatre with wire wound so tightly round their muzzles that their mouths bled, their noses blocked with a thick discharge so that their breathing was difficult.
>
> A surgeon cut into one dog's groin without anaesthetic in an attempt to find the femoral vein. The incision was about three inches long. For about three minutes the surgeon separated the muscle layers as he searched for the vein. When he found it he bled the dog to death. During this procedure the dog 'vocalized' its pain and distress but neither doctors or nurses showed any sign of pity or discomfort. In fact I remember one pretty nurse shouting to be heard above the cries of the dog, asking me to describe my wedding-dress. When enough blood had been obtained to prime the extra-corporeal circulation machine needed for the operation, one dog remained alive and conscious. I followed the attendant who removed it to the incinerator and threw it in.

Dogs are the raw material of literally millions of such experiments from Greece to Russia, from the USA to Japan. One university in Tokyo alone uses 1,000 dogs *per month*. To supply this demand Japan imports dogs from all over the world, but specially from the dog-breeding, animal-loving British Isles. In April 1969 the *People* sent a special reporter to investigate the conditions under which thousands of British dogs and puppies were exported, some ostensibly for pets and for breeding, but largely as laboratory fodder. What upset the *People*'s reporter so much and his readers even more were the conditions under which the laboratory animals were kept, the complete lack of care and of any effort to finish their lives off humanely. What seemed clear from this exposure, and was confirmed to us by a member of Crufts, was that the dogs were 'big business' and that this was a flourishing, lucrative export trade.

Eighteen months before the *People*'s crusade on behalf of British dogs exported to the other side of the world to untold misery and lingering death, we had eye-witness accounts from anti-vivisection societies and pictures which were confirmed by later photographs taken especially for the *People*.

No one who has ever owned a dog can have any doubts about their capacity for suffering, nor the ills they are heir to when kept in tiny cubicles in their own ordure, with wire hawsers cutting into their necks.

And if such experiments (if not such experimental *conditions*) are really useful to help suffering mankind and we try to find some alternative, what can replace them?

Well, it has been pointed out that some of the most important discoveries of modern medicine were made without the sufferings of animals at all. Penicillin is cited and the use of iodine in thyroid disease. The infectious diseases have largely been brought under control (and in Europe all but conquered) by improvements in sanitation, cleanliness and nutrition. Louis Pasteur emphasized that it was more important to prevent disease than to treat it, and diseases such as typhoid, cholera, and many kinds of plague have been controlled more by prevention than by cure.

An increasing number of doctors appear to be dubious about the validity of results obtained from experiments on animals. The *Journal of Physiology* for September 1959 reports:

Dogs were put in steel boxes and subjected to carbon monoxide poisoning. After a short time they began to stagger, and some of them vomited. Then they fell or lay down and became unconscious. They were left in boxes for half an hour after losing consciousness, the aim being to take them as near death as possible. In fact, four were dead when removed from the exposure box, and six more died soon afterwards. Four others later developed pneumonia and died, and another became permanently blind. Altogether, fifty-nine dogs were used in these experiments which, according to Dr Beddow Bayly, threw *little or no fresh light* on the problem of carbon monoxide poisoning, which had already been the subject of many experiments on animals over a long period of time.

Experiments performed on twelve bitches at the Department of Physiology, University of Edinburgh, were described in the *Journal of Physiology*, Volume 145, No. 2, March 3rd 1959. The perineum was split and a catheter was passed into the bladder. A large dose of water had already been given some three hours before the experiment. Diuresis was induced by introducing more water through a stomach tube. Samples of urine and of blood taken from veins, were analysed and measured. Stilboestrol was then injected and the measurements were retaken and compared with the first. In some dogs, operations on the pituitary gland and hypothalamus had been performed through the mouth under anaesthesia; in others the ovaries or testicles had been removed. These procedures and observations in severely mutilated dogs lasted from eight to eleven days, during the greater part of which time they were conscious. *The results were inconclusive.* [our italics.]

# 12

# *The Shrinking World of Nature*

We spray the fields and scatter
The poison on the land,
So that no wicked wild flowers
Upon our farms are found.
We like whatever helps us
To line our purse with pence,
The twenty-four hour broiler-house
And sweet electric fence.

JOHN BETJEMAN

It was the outcry following the Tennessee Valley 'dust-bowl' calamity that first made the man in the street aware that erosion was not just a technical term used by geographers or soil-structure specialists. But the publicity given this misuse of one particular area of the earth's surface has not prevented similar conditions and situations arising elsewhere. We are now more aware of the dangers of creating such dust-bowls, but expediency, the pursuit of profit, and the constant reduction of overheads and man-hours would still appear to exert stronger pressures. So dust storms sweep across prairie farms in North America, Canada, Australia and South America, tearing the heart out of the precious topsoil and scattering its potential fertility to the four winds, so that, as in the case of Tennessee, once productive valleys become deserts.

Even in Britain, a country possessing a high average rainfall, with trees and sheltering hedges grubbed out in the interests of more efficient agriculture, the top soil blows off. In March 1968 a series of dust storms affected East Anglia and parts of Nottinghamshire, Lincoln and Huntingdon. These so-called 'black-blizzards' spread far beyond their more usual boundaries of flat fen-land. Schools were closed, lights came on at 2 p.m., and traffic slowed to a crawl with headlights full on in daylight. Farmers lost acres of newly-planted crops, spring-drilled seed disappeared overnight, flying grit particles shredded new spring foliage, while streams, ditches and irrigation canals filled up with powdered soil.

Ministry of Agriculture improvement grants have encouraged farmers to rip out 10,000 *miles* of hedges each year. This enables the heavy machinery used in modern cultivation to operate in long, time-saving lines. Yet hedged land supports at least thirty different kinds of birds, where unhedged it may give homes to only three or four. The 'pocket-handkerchief' fields which made up the patchwork quilt of our countryside are uneconomic in the new farming. Furthermore the labour of spreading 'muck' on the land from livestock which is largely contained in factory-like buildings, is more costly than the use of manufactured artificial manures. Road-widening, building, drainage schemes and the 'improved layout' of farmlands all combine to induce a widespread felling of trees, which in turn contributes to the dust-bowl effect. Our passion for tidiness, for eliminating nature or at least disciplining her, does not give the natural regeneration of hedges and verges any chance. Mechanical hedgecutters and verge-trimmers cut off saplings before they can establish growth, and similarly many wild plants, including herbs and flowers, are cut so frequently and often at the wrong season, that they eventually disappear altogether. We have seen this happen in the case of primroses and violets, once common in most English hedgebanks, while the rarer wayside plants have completely vanished.

The oak, a typical hedgerow tree, with great regenerative powers of its own, is disappearing from the British countryside (of which it is a symbol adopted by the National Trust) at the rate of 100,000 trees each year. Oaks play a vital part in supporting life. One tree can provide nests for twenty different species of bird and over 500 species of insect. The invaluable soil-building earthworm enriches the land by digesting the tree's fallen leaves. It has been estimated that an average mature tree may have 200,000 leaves.

As the trees are felled, to clear land for building, or for the timber and expensive veneers they can provide, or in the interests of more efficient husbandry, all this habitat is lost to the birds and insects which once they supported. In addition, marshland is drained and heaths ploughed while mixed deciduous woodland is grubbed out and replaced with quick-growing conifers. Chalk downlands vanish together with their thorn and juniper bushes, waste land is cleared of gorse and whins and in the interest of building sites or prairie type cultivations the homes of countless insects, butterflies, birds, and small creatures, are destroyed. So the whole natural ecology of an area is deranged and broken, resulting in the impoverishment of wild life, then the rarity and ultimately the complete disappearance of innumerable species.

The felling of great oak woods and other clearances would not matter quite so much if we could be persuaded to leave lesser patches of uncultivated ground as oases in the midst of the deserts we are creating.

The British press have not been slow to record present trends in the countryside, and features and supplements on how we are using or abusing nature appear quite regularly. In April 1969, the *Observer* magazine charted the rise and fall of Britain's wild life with an exhortation to conservation. Such features stress that man's effort to tidy and tame wild nature is beginning to have dire effects. The tidying up is not confined to burning and cutting, for now most powerful chemicals have come to aid us in our fight against untidy nature. 'Farming Notes' in *The Times* of 3 March 1969 observed:

> The hedgeless, treeless, level stretch of cropped land which seems to be the farming ideal is not exactly hospitable to wild life. Indiscriminate use of pesticides, unnecessary spraying of small weeds were often undertaken without thought to the birds, insects and flora they harboured.

It was also pointed out that the hazards of aerial spraying were often not fully understood and that abandoned chemical containers thrown into ditches and ponds often resulted in a release of chemical residues which killed frogs, tadpoles and newts. The increasing rarity of bumblebees and grasshoppers was also commented upon.

The destruction of hedges and trees is perhaps the most easily recognized loss of habitat, the most spectacular and the most accurately documented. It takes but a few minutes with modern equipment to fell a forest giant which needed two or three centuries to grow. To replace its capacity for timber will, under similar conditions, take the same length of time. The rate of deafforestation increases almost daily. America by itself consumes more than six million tons of wood for newsprint alone. Such prodigality repeated throughout the increasingly literate countries of the world must result in an ever-increasing loss of habitat for wild life of every kind. In Britain a landowner may fell up to one hundred grown trees each year, without reference to any authority. (This is the cubic footage of felling allowed, translated into terms of actual trees.) After this, application for a felling licence is required; whether it be granted or not, considerable inroads into our arboriculture have already been made.

It has been concluded that the minimum tree cover should be 33 per cent of total surface area. Sweden can claim 63 per cent, Germany 26 per cent and France 25 per cent. Britain, which to some of us may still appear fairly well wooded, has only $6\frac{1}{2}$ per cent. In France, as one tree is felled, from four to six are planted to allow for failure, and to help to provide increasing cover.

In Britain it was claimed that in 1945 the ratio of hedgerow to land was something like 70 miles to every 5,000 acres. By 1963 the mileage of hedgerow had dwindled to 46 to the same acreage and by March 1968 it was down to the frightening figure of only 14·6 miles.

During the last five years alone, a total of something like 40,000 miles of hedges have been lost, and in one district under survey 71 per cent of the total length of hedge existing in 1962 had been destroyed. Oaks disappear at the rate of 10,000 trees a year, from hedges and copses. The replacement is at the low rate of three saplings for every one hundred mature trees. Such massive destruction of the homes of countless insects, birds and small mammals, has resulted in the decimation of whole species and the increasing rarity of those which not long ago were quite common.

Equal enemy with the mechanical saw and bulldozer are the scientist and the scientific firm's salesmen who offer short cuts to the farmer or the market gardener and the local authority for 'tidying up' untidy nature.

A new spray promises complete 'brushwood control' and advertising pressure exhorts us to remove and eradicate 'briars and brambles'. A basal bark spray will control 'common scrub species' such as birch, hazel and willow gorse and broom, as well as ivy and nettles. Guelder rose, the ruddy twigs of the dogwood, spindle, rowan, holly, whitebeam, blackthorn and whitethorn are all vital to bird populations and are all victims of the new scrub eliminators. The bramble and thorn mask the earths of foxes and the setts of badgers and offer cover to small rodents, all part of a food chain in nature.

A spokesman for the Protection of Livestock Association has stated:

> It would appear that many people today are of the impression that all birds and animals other than those needed for the immediate food of man have no right on earth whatsoever. Yet many creatures do incalculable good.

A recent catalogue sent us from one of the great chemical and veterinary firms in Britain offered us poison sprays which will eliminate the following 'weeds': Forget-me-not, black and white mustard, buttercup, cranesbill, chickweed, scarlet pimpernel, fools parsley, shepherds purse, dock, soft rush, groundsel, dandelion, plantain, speedwell, mayweed, bugloss, fumitory, poppy, chamomile, campion, daisy, sorrel, wild radish, penny cress and orache. It will be noted that on this list appear many plants which are devoured by wild birds, poultry and herbivorous mammals. Some of the plants on this list to be eradicated have pharmaceutical, toiletry and herbalist value also. During the last war Italian prisoners on British farms often varied their rations by picking wild flowers and herbs which their more 'advanced' employers had forgotten were of any value to man or beast. Mr Rolf Gardiner, well-known landowner and conservationist wrote in the *Farmer's Weekly* in 1967 of the biological need for trees and hedgerows:

> It is not only the preservationists who want to retain the patterns of what is considered typical English countryside, but the naturalists who see a continuous impoverishment of wild life, flora and fauna following in the wake of economic agriculture and modern farming practice with chemical sprays, herbicides and "artificials". There is an extraordinary anomaly in that two government departments, the Ministry of Agriculture and the Ministry of Land and Natural Resources (responsible for the maintenance of the countryside) are following two unreconciled and opposed grant-giving policies.

Mr Gardiner went on to write of Professor Alwin Seifert, the German specialist in landscape and organic gardening, who showed him orchards and fruit farms never treated with poison sprays, yet producing fine unblemished fruit and unpoisoned blossom for bees. Hedges of willow, (whose catkins gave the bees their first springtime nourishment) limes, ash and sycamore abounded in this Bavarian countryside with a healthy agriculture. Seifert pointed out that at least 5 per cent of such farmland should be kept under indigenous shrub and tree cover. Mr Gardiner commented on the Lincolnshire farming friend who bulldozed all his hedgerows to make a prairie for corn and sugar-beet, but, after some experience of the dust-bowl conditions that followed, was busy planting shelter belts again for dear life.

We still do not know enough about the long-term effects of such a wholesale interference in our ecology, and the belief that the answer to everything lies in a spray and yet another and stronger spray, may be a lethal danger to all living things, which includes man himself.

Rachel Carson, in *Silent Spring*, describes what happened in forests sprayed by the United States Forest Service in 1956. Some 885,000 acres of forested lands were sprayed with DDT. 'The intention was to control the spruce budworm, instead it released a plague of spider mites which affected the sprayed areas but nowhere else.' Similar results had been noted in the Yellowstone Park and later in New Mexico. It was then realized that the similarity of the cases was not coincidental. The chemical sprays killed off the various predators of the spider mite who were not themselves sensitive. So in curing one evil, a larger was let loose. Miss Carson records that in a famous apple growing area of Virginia DDT spraying to improve the crop resulted in a plague of red-banded leaf-rollers. So in *protecting* his crops the scientifically-minded fruit grower found that the cure was more damaging than the original 'pest'. Rachel Carson points out that 'We are seldom aware of the protection afforded by natural enemies until it fails.'

Interference in the natural order to promote more efficient land-use is not confined to the control of insects. In the United States the farmers' zeal in exterminating the coyote resulted in plagues of field mice which the coyote had controlled as its staple food. Similarly, in Britain, wholesale destruction of foxes, particularly in non-hunting areas, has resulted in great increases in rats and mice. In Arizona the deer population was kept in check by its predators, which included wolves and pumas; but with man slaughtering the predators, the deer increased beyond the resources of their environment which began to be damaged and destroyed in their efforts to find food. Predatory insects of the field and forest play the same kind of role in their own environment. Seventy to eighty per cent of the total of all the world's creatures are insects, and by providing food for countless birds and small mammals they are a most important link in the environmental chain.

In the United States (to be followed later in Britain and elsewhere) the search for stronger insecticides to protect crops resulted in the use of sodium selenate, the first 'systemic insecticide', which permeates the tissue of plants and animals alike, rendering them toxic. Peas, beans, sugar beet and cottonseed were soaked or coated with this chemical. One of the results was that bees feeding on the flowering plants obtained contaminated nectar. Where birds ate the insects which had been poisoned by contact with contaminated plants, the result was not always sudden death. Sterility, eggs that would not hatch, or that when opened revealed two-headed monstrosities, were the initial outcome of the new insecticides and sprays.

In Britain especially, the birds of prey, including the rarer kinds, after feeding on such contaminated birds or their eggs, received the full build-up of poisons in their systems. Hawks, falcons, buzzards and even eagles became victims of the poison train. DDT having been replaced by all-purpose sprays aimed at higher yields and a 'tidier' countryside, such as dieldrin, aldrin and hephachlor (aimed at combating soil-insects), reports of increased casualties began to come in. Newly-dressed corn killed many partridges and game birds of the arable lands, the untimely death of Britain's game caused quite a stir. Questions were asked in Parliament and heated correspondence broke out in the sporting and farming journals. A joint report by the Royal Society for the Protection of Birds and the British Trust for Ornithology recorded sixty-seven different kinds of bird that had been killed by treated seed-dressings or toxic sprays. The Nature Conservancy were concerned at the decimation of kestrels and other birds of prey, particularly after the great trouble taken to encourage the nesting and breeding of ospreys in Scotland.

A scientific count on a Lincolnshire estate revealed partridge and greenfinch and both long-eared and tawny owls to be among the casualties. On a Cambridge estate, a count yielded 4,000 assorted corpses, 83 of them game birds. This brought the Game Research Association to join the bird societies in their enquiry into the effects of toxic chemicals being used in such a widespread fashion over British farmlands. Foxes, too, began to suffer, probably as the result of picking up contaminated pigeons and other items of food, as the poison spread through the chain from seed to bird, and from bird to predator. It was estimated that over 1,000 foxes died in just six months from chlorinated hydracarbon poisoning, and for a short space hunting was suspended.

The House of Commons was pressed to prohibit the more toxic chemicals, and farmers agreed to exercise restraint and not seek all their salvation at the end of a spray nozzle. But many species have never truly recovered from the full force of the highest poisoning period.

Rachel Carson has emphasized what experience has proved all too true, that insecticides are not really selective, although they may be produced as being so. They are deadly poisons and can be taken by friend and foe alike. Death by poison is cruel and very distressing to watch and there is no alleviation. The dying foxes suffered severe convulsions, small birds could not fly but staggered about on the ground, small rodents were found with their mouths full of dirt as if they had been biting the ground in agony. Rachel Carson from her own observation asked, 'By acquiescing in an act that can cause such suffering to a living creature, who among us is not diminished as a human being?'

But almost a decade has passed since she wrote, and profit still supercedes humane consideration. Only when profit or sport are threatened, will effective action be taken, and until his pocket is affected, mankind will continue to use the poison sprays and ignore conscience, or moral questions.

Pollution takes many forms, and even after the initial scares and checks on the use of such poisons as dieldrin, aldrin and heptachlor, suspicion began to fall upon other substances. A so-called safe pesticide, yBHC, had escaped control because little of it had been found as residue in the livers of dead birds. It has since been found that unless the livers were examined immediately after death, the chemical could not be detected in analysis, but experimental pigeons fed with yBHC in their diet died within six days, and this too came under the heading of pesticides about whose long-term effects we simply have not enough knowledge. For long the myth was propagated that herbicides were toxic only to plants and in no way threatened wild life, but with arsenical sprays the Ministry of Agriculture have to warn against going into newly sprayed fields, that protective clothing must be worn by operators, and that no food must be eaten on the site unless it is well wrapped and unless there are facilities for thorough washing before handling. Wild life and even cattle have been victims of this type of spraying. Only after several operators had been seriously ill and the death of one farmer's wife had been directly attributed to this type of spray was it banned, and supplies called in. But, having proved so toxic to human beings, its effect on lesser forms of life are not hard to imagine. The emergence of species of insect or 'pest' or weed which has proved immune to spraying results in ever deadlier chemicals being employed. The malaria mosquito has become resistant to DDT and now to dieldrin. Nature has proliferated in great variety with inbuilt checks and balances.

In Britain the rabbit plague known as myxomatosis was spread purposely (and at first illegally) by farmers and graziers anxious to rid their pastures of a ravenous pest. This resulted in much suffering, and during the late 1940s and early 1950s there was the frequent sight of swollen, blinded, half-stupefied rabbits dragging out their miserable lives before death or some humane passer-by ended their sufferings. But slowly, over the years, some kind of immunity has been bred among the survivors, and we now have both the rabbit and the disease.

In little more than two decades, synthetic substances have been deposited and distributed all over the natural world so that they now occur virtually everywhere and nowhere is immune, although we still do not know enough about their effects on the world of nature, which is in the long run also the world of man.

Residues of poisonous chemicals linger in the soil, get absorbed into the bodies of insects and animals, find their way into our river systems and lodge in the tissues of fish and reptiles. Traces are found in underground river systems and in our seas from pole to pole. They are now so universal that scientists carrying out animal experiments find it almost impossible to find any subjects totally free from contamination and have taken to breeding specimens in air-conditioned, pollution-free, sterilized chambers.

One of the things we are learning painfully and quite possibly too late is that many of these chemicals are of enormous biological potency, which by manipulation of molecules can change, build up, or increase their effects when combined in living tissue in the most sinister and often deadly ways. Their molecular structure alters when combined with fat, or upon entering our water supplies, so that their poisons do not diminish but are transmuted and quite often increased.

Dr W. C. Hueper of the National Cancer Institute writes: 'Anyone who has watched the dusters and sprayers of insecticides at work must have been impressed by the almost supreme carelessness with which poisonous substances are dispensed'. Certainly we have seen widespread drifting from crop-sprayers and witnessed dressings administered from the air even in windless conditions fall beyond the boundaries of the fields to be sprayed.

Crops dusted with DDT end as meal fed to hens and cattle, resulting in eggs, milk and butter which are part of a chain reaction so that what began as a tiny quantity may end up as a heavy concentration. Hephtachlor and dieldrin are about five times as toxic as DDT when swallowed, and as much as forty times so when absorbed by the skin. Aldrin is lethal enough for a portion the size of an aspirin tablet to be sufficient to kill 400 quail. Endrin is the most toxic of all the hydrocarbons, being five times more poisonous than dieldrin and fifteen times as poisonous to mammals, three hundred times to some birds and as much as thirty times to fish.

Parathion is one of the more widely used of the organic phosphates. Bees coming into contact with it usually die within the hour. About seven million pounds of parathion is applied to orchards and fields in the USA annually by every kind of equipment from handblowers to spray-planes.

Applied to the land, toxic chemicals spread by wind and drainage and rain fall into rivers and then the oceans, become incorporated in the plankton and further accumulated in the fish which eat it, and so the chain continues.

Meanwhile, if an animal is a 'pest', nothing is too bad for it. With foxes being destroyed by strychnine, trapping, hunting and shooting,

the rats which the foxes ate in such large quantities began to proliferate. Warfarin, a comparatively humane poison and not usually thought
to be deadly to pets, was too slow, as it involved prebaiting, and in
addition rats in parts of Wales were developing some kind of immunity
against it. So red squill, sodium fluoro-acetate, and other rodenticides
containing elemental phosphorus were called into service. The
University Federation for Animal Welfare describes these poisons as
being the ultimate in cruelty – animals literally tortured for six or seven
days, rolled over in agony, suffering slow asphyxiation and convulsions.
But the Industrial Pest Control Association and the scientific directors
of large rodenticide manufacturers strongly oppose any ban on the use
of these poisons.

In 1968 the case of contaminated mussels, stretching from south east
Scotland to Hull, hit the headlines. Commercial collection of mussels had
to be stopped because of the risk to human life. No explanation of the
cause of the outbreak was ever offered, and again this may be some leak
of chemical or combination of chemicals which when mixed with water
increases its effect and builds up into an insidious and dangerous matter.

The oceans of the world are now at the receiving end of pollution
by every scientific poison that twentieth-century man has devised in
his short cut to getting rich quick and bringing nature under his
complete domination. Radioactive waste, effluent from atomic energy
reactors, radium and cobalt waste from hospitals, nuclear fallout,
chemical wastes from industry and residues of sprays from farm,
garden and forest, find their way into the world's water systems,
combining to form as yet unresearched compounds with possibly
disastrous long-term effects. A deluge of chemical pollution now
descends on the rivers and seas, some applied deliberately to destroy
undesirable plants, weeds or insects. The accumulation of toxic chemicals from so many different sources cannot adequately be measured.
What is certain is that nowhere escapes the menace. Tests reveal that
areas far from the source of pollution contain DDT. Ocean currents,
winds, migrating birds and fishes render it impossible to contain the
contamination.

In eastern Canada, where DDT had been sprayed from the air at the
rate of half a pound to the acre in a solution of oil, the Miramichi
salmon runs were ruined, dead and dying fish were found, and all the
river life on which the trout and salmon depended – larvae, and insects
– was destroyed. In Maine, the Department of Inland Fisheries
reported moribund suckers exhibiting typical symptoms of DDT
poisoning. Fish exhibited tremors and spasms, and trout, blind

168

and dying, were floating downstream to carry their poison-laden remains further afield and eventually out to sea.

And if DDT is so lethal, some of the other poisons, notably the chlorides, chlorates, Phosphoric acid salts and fluorides, combine in water with as yet unknown results. Deformed fish, infertile spawn, contaminated fishing grounds, are only just beginning to tell a story for whose ending the most sanguine mind can only find foreboding.

In the USA the casualties among river fish and the reported loss of frogs and other pond-life led the American Society of Ichthyologists and Herpetologists to pass a resolution calling on the Department of Agriculture to cease 'aerial distribution of heptachlor, dieldrin and equivalent poisons, before irreparable harm is done.'

Frogs and toads have almost vanished from the more populous areas of the British Isles. The old assumption that science has the answer to everything is ironically called in question by the scientists themselves complaining about the shortage of frogs and squids which are the raw materials of so many biological experiments. When our rivers and lakes became coated with detergent foam, manufacturers agreed to modify their products sufficiently to cut down on this particular type of water pollution. But, having taken action over the household detergents, our waterways next became faced with a totally new pollution known as eutrophication, or the overloading of water with artificial nutrients, mostly the nitrates and super-phosphates of intensive farming. These act as manures and growth stimulants to algae, always present in fresh-water lakes. In Somerset, the Chew Valley reservoir, a recent man-made lake noted for the excellence of its trout and the abundance of its bird life, was suddenly transformed by eutrophication, which had already turned Lake Erie in Canada into a stagnant cesspit. It has been stated that the nitrate content of some English drinking water is now so high that it constitutes a real danger to babies and young children. If this is so, the result on other forms of life which drink it will also be anything but beneficial.

Drinking water for humans has at least gone through many purifying processes before it emerges from the tap. Wild life is on the receiving end of undiluted chemicals. And the use of nitrogen is still rising. Statistics produced by the Fertilizer Manufacturers Association reveal a rise of 9.1 per cent in the use of nitrogen during 1968—the amount having risen steadily for the ten previous years.

Albert Schweitzer pointed out the danger when he wrote:

Man has lost the capacity to foresee and forestall. He will end by destroying the earth.

In August 1968, the first woman president of the British Association, Professor Dame Kathleen Lonsdale, addressed her audience on 'Science and the Good Life'. She echoes Schweitzer with the words: 'Science, if not a monster, is, in fact, at best a victim of man's determination to destroy himself and his inheritance.' She reminded the Association that 'knowledge and privilege bring great responsibilities and that many of the countries that ask for jet fighters need water and irrigation systems far more.' Her summing up refers to human life but equally applies to all living things under man's uncertain, half-understood dominion:

> The responsible use of science will enhance the quality of life. The irresponsible use could quench human life as we know it.

# 13

# *In Conclusion*

The dilemma of modern man lies in his innate confusion with regard to his own place in nature. His desire to dominate all other forms of life leads to destruction rather than co-operation. He both hates and fears the wild life that occupied this earth so long before he appeared on the scene, and yet he cannot live without it. Man owes his survival to the whole complex structure of nature, without which he cannot exist, and yet he has been conditioned and the whole of his upbringing has been aimed at teaching him to think that he is superior to the rest of creation, and can impose his will upon it as he chooses. His confusion exists in his need of, and utter dependence upon, the very creatures he seeks to dominate and destroy.

Technological man can alter or destroy what has taken millions of years to evolve. In a few short seasons he reduced the Tennessee valley to a dust-bowl and then had to import thousands of earthworms to restore life to the area. So much does man depend on what he may popularly consider to be the meanest of creatures, for his life's continuance. Without the lowly, unlovable earthworm the whole structure of fertility would cease to exist, and our civilization is built on this natural basis which we ignore at our peril.

The assumption that the lesser creation was made and sent entirely for man's benefit is paraded wherever animals are misused, exploited or treated like 'things'. And if man as a whole is confused in his attitudes, individual nations are no less so. Ambivalent attitudes towards cruelty to animals exist everywhere in spite of some progress, and no one nation is entirely blameless or entirely guilty in the exercise of their dominion over the natural world.

The British, who like to think of themselves as a nation of animal-lovers, have their blind spots. The critics of bloodsports, which are so much part of the British upper-class tradition, may be forgiven for thinking that our great humane society should add another S to its title and become, more truthfully, the Royal Society for the Prevention of Cruelty to *Some* Animals. Such critics should remember that the Society can only act within the law, and that while the man in the street can be punished for setting his dogs to chase and kill a neigh-bour's cat, the hunt is a law unto itself. Until the law is changed, cruel incidents in stag, hare, otter and even fox-hunting are not illegal, merely regrettable.

In 1969 an RSPCA inspector gained much publicity on resigning his job because he said it consisted almost entirely of slaughtering un-wanted dogs, most of them young and fit. A few miles away a large, well-run dogs' home in the depth of the country was closed because residents of an adjacent village complained of the noise of barking. In court, the complainants all declared that they were animal lovers and owned dogs themselves. The residents who supported the dogs' home and declared that the barking was not a nuisance were disregarded.

The British are not alone in what might be termed their hypocritical attitudes to animal cruelty. Denmark, while prohibiting that refinement of cruelty, the chained dog, originated the sweat-box system for pig management, and while condemning methods of training performing animals, is the largest exporter of horses for meat (with all the suffering that entails) in Europe.

Sweden, long held up as an example for its enlightened attitude towards animal welfare, possesses huge resources for animal experi-mentation and vivisection. And when the controversial film, *A Plague on Our Children*, was made for British television, evidence of micro-biological warfare experiments on animals was obtained in Sweden.

The Netherlands, pioneers of intensive veal units and among the foremost dealers in ponies for meat, ban hunting with hounds and in fact all killing for sport except shooting, for which a special licence is necessary.

Canada, with some of the tightest laws for the protection of domestic animals, has one of the worst records for cruelty inherent in fur trapping and sealing. Spain, with its record of bullfighting and its callous treatment of work animals, yet lent its weight to the recom-mendations of the International Society for the Protection of Animals with regard to cruelty to wild birds in Belgium. Similarly, Uruguay, with its sad history of horse exports to Europe, often under the worst possible conditions, joined in an international protest to Japan with regard to introducing bullfighting to Tokyo.

But if bullfighting is frowned upon as an imported sport, it is shrugged off as part of a national culture in the lands of its origin. By the same token fox-hunting is a recognized part of 'Merrie England', as the popularity of hunting scenes on Christmas cards and table mats in Britain testifies.

The United States of America, with the highest churchgoing population of any Christian country in the world today, possesses few states with laws to protect animals from experimentation or vivisection. California is one exception. In fact, in the name of progress, anything goes. This is illogical, for Professor J. G. Lawler, Professor of Humanities in St Xavier College of Chicago, points out that the rights of animals should be a supremely Christian concern:

> Any question of theology and animals must broach the question of vivisection. Many twentieth century Christians and even some Roman Catholics have found it almost impossible to understand why the animal, which according to traditional opinion, has no other life, can be forced to suffer in that one life in order to extend or preserve the temporal life of man, which in the Christian conception is merely the prelude to eternal life.

In France, St Hubert wins hands down over St Francis, and the blessing of staghounds is the accepted thing, so much so that when one curé refused this office it made headline news.

Many countries and creeds produce rebels against orthodox indifference. Such a man was Professor Dr Johannes Ude who spoke on the church and animal welfare, referring to the 'crime of vivisection' at Goettingen, in Germany, in 1958. In 1944 he had been arrested for preaching against Hitler's Reich, and as a Christian he had protested against the Nazi persecution of the Jews.

In the 1960s the first ever 'animal welfare pilgrimage' left London for Lourdes, organized by the Catholic Study Circle for Animal Welfare led by Father Basil Wright, who is the acting editor of the Circle's bulletin, *The Ark*. He expressed the hope that a permanent 'international information kiosk for animal welfare in Lourdes might be manned in turn by representatives of kindred societies from other countries.' A step in the right direction from a church which does not believe that animals have souls.

The Buddhist's belief that all life is sacred, while excellent in concept, is often cruel in practice, where too many beasts exist with too little 'keep' or veterinary attention and so the religion most against cruelty often displays starvation and suffering on as large a scale as any other less enlightened.

Perhaps the most consistent of religious bodies are the Quakers. The Society of Friends produced Ruth Harrison with her long and uphill battle to obtain humane conditions for our farm and food animals. All through the long fight for animal legislation, the Quakers have come out strongly with the reformers. They quote Albert Schweitzer's 'Until we extend the circumference of our circle of compassion to every living creature, we shall never enjoy world peace', and they condemn vivisection with the statement that 'good never comes out of evil in any way whatsoever'. On 4 October 1967 a delegation of churches, which included Ruth Harrison, presented a petition to Pope Paul VI, begging his blessing 'on our efforts to forward a merciful and intelligent treatment of the animals created by God for His Glory'.

The petition, which covered all amusements based on the 'baiting and killing of animals' and referred to the 'training and exploitation of performing animals', was organized by the Catholic Study Circle. This Animal Welfare Pilgrimage to Rome, from 30 September to 7 October, so including the feast of St Francis, was a signal for all Christian denominations to combine. The Church of England was led by the Bishop of Worcester, Canon Edward Carpenter and Sir George Trevelyan, the Methodists by the Rev. The Lord Soper, the Catholic by the Rt. Rev. Mgr. John Barton, DD and the Rev. Dom Ambrose Aguis, OSB. The pilgrimate received world-wide coverage and the Pope gave his blessing.

Children can be notoriously cruel, possibly to compensate for some of the domination and bullying by grown-ups, but there is no doubt that many children have a sadistic streak which shows itself in their treatment of animals. Perhaps the child or children who were responsible for hammering six-inch nails into a dog's shoulder-bone (as reported by the Scottish Society for the Prevention of Vivisection in 1967) were abnormal. The late Gilbert Harding commented on the number of stray cats caught and killed by children to provide 'Davy Crockett' headgear when that character was all the rage. And if adults can get 'kicks' out of cruelty, so can children, without knowing that awakening sexual urges experienced at puberty, demand some form of positive expression.

A reported case of boys setting a squirrel alight came to our notice at the same time as a fox destruction society fired an area of gorse and scrub cliff to destroy their quarry, some of which were most certainly burnt alive. And the child who watches his father beat the harmless grass snake to death may be forgiven for thinking that he may do the same with impunity.

The country child may treat animals badly with a kick or a blow because he sees farmworkers acting that way, and because familiarity breeds contempt. The town child may neglect his pets because he does not properly understand their needs, and his parents, far removed from nature, do not really want the intrusion of alien life into their neat modern homes.

Humane education is the answer, and the humane societies, particularly the RSPCA, do their best with leaflets on every aspect of domestic animals, from keeping fish to the proper treatment of tortoises. But unless the parents or teachers are interested, such information may never come the child's way.

Children who are unduly sensitive to pain or to the ill-treatment of animals run the risk of being thought soft in a world where toughness is the 'in' thing. And the adult who really cares, and is seen to care, how his food is produced and killed, how 'pests' are controlled or how animals are used in the name of science and progress, runs the risk of being classed as the worst kind of crank. For no crank is more reviled than the 'animal crank'. Journalists and television interviewers delight in 'taking the mickey' out of anyone who actively opposes cruelty or tries to do anything for animals, and the adjective 'sentimental' is never far from the lips of the critics of all would-be reformers. 'Do-gooding' has become a suspect phrase, and kindness to animals is often held up as a sublimation of other natural instincts.

But the betterment of conditions for oppressed minorities has always been left to 'cranks' who, from the abolition of the slave trade onwards, have been told that ruin would attend their humane reform. If progress towards humane reform is slow and uncertain, this is partly because the public is uninformed and often told only what vested interests would have them know. Often the only choice for the layman is between largely ineffectual forms of protest—picketing of circuses, parading with anti-bloodsports banners and slogans at Boxing Day meets, and sitting down outside large factory farms—and a sophisticated kind of indifference which is much less 'anti-social'. Protest may indeed hinder progress by the very fact that it advertises liberality and reform, without proceeding to positive action. Hence, enquiries and committees and royal commissions can lull public opinion into thinking that something is being accomplished, although not one animal may be saved or helped thereby.

Meanwhile it is easier to use the epithet 'crank' than to give serious consideration to popular attitudes. Yet by this same token many of the wisest and most revered minds throughout the ages of man's evolution could be classified as cranks on account of their abhorrence of cruelty to the lesser creation, and of the ill effect of the practice of it on man himself.

Consider Cicero's 'no cruelty is useful', and Shaw's 'Cruelty begets its offspring—war'. Moses' law stressed the need for humane treatment of animals, exhorting us not to muzzle the ox that treads out the corn and to ensure that all beasts of burden should have one day of rest, while Solomon stated unequivocally that 'the righteous man shall have regard to the life of his beast'.

Zoroaster, as early as 600 BC, laid emphasis on the fact that God created animals as well as man and that no sacrifice will atone for a bad deed—only a good deed will do. Jainism, in India, takes into consideration the rights of animals and founds 'hospitals' for them.

St John Chrysostom in AD 370 argued 'surely we ought to show them great kindness and gentleness for many reasons but above all because they are of the same origins as ourselves'. A few years earlier, St Basil of Caesarea, who founded the Liturgy, prayed 'Enlarge within us the sense of fellowship with all living things, our brothers, the animals'.

He is joined by St Jerome, taking the thorn from the lion's paw, by St Malo, St Colomba, St Cuthbert, with his seals of Lindisfarne, and St Francis of Assisi, in his regard for the brute creation.

John Wesley could bring himself to express the hope 'that something better remains after death for these poor creatures'.

Saints, philosophers, thinkers, artists—Buddha, Plato, Plutarch, Pythagoras, Leonardo da Vinci, Shelley, Thoreau, Swedenborg, Gandhi, Porphyry and Schweitzer—are all 'cranks' by the anti-animal-welfare standard.

Gandhi called vivisection 'the blackest spot of civilization', while Victor Hugo described it as 'a crime against creation'.

Da Vinci in his diaries reveals how he bought caged birds in order to set them free, and comments on man as 'always warring with his own species, persecuting, harassing and devastating all things that are on the earth and beneath it in the waters'. If he were writing today, would he be hailed as a great mind, a thinker, inventor, artist and innovator, or would he be classified as a crank?

Jeremy Bentham in 1718 could declare that 'cruelty to animals should be classed among crimes cognisable by law'. As far back as 348

BC. Aristotle could proclaim that animals were acutely sensitive to pain, yet a Minister of State and spokesman for the House of Lords in 1969 could decide that to protect animals from being exported to foreign laboratories would be a 'considerable disservice to science'.

Men as diverse as Luther and Axel Munthe could spare time and energy to defend the animal and bird kingdoms against the cruelties of the human race. Schopenhauer could exclaim, 'he who is cruel to animals is no good to man'. Ruskin pointed out that 'He who is not actively kind, is cruel', which is echoed by Burke's 'all that is necessary for the triumph of evil is that good men do nothing'.

Nearer to our own time, a former Governor of Maine, P. P. Baxter, wrote that 'kindness is the noblest trait of human nature, cruelty the meanest and lowest. In giving man absolute power over the creatures beneath him the Creator put humans to the test and gave them the choice of kindness or cruelty, of good or evil'. Yet Richard Martin, the greatest instigator of humane reform, described by Sir Jonah Barrington as having 'benevolence towards men and humanity towards the brute creation', was designated in his *Times* obituary of 1834 as 'the late eccentric', while Chambers *Dictionary of Biography* for 1899 vouchsafed him not a single line.

In the third century AD, Porphyry could write:

> From mere wantonness, from licentiousness, men cruelly murder, in sport, in the hunting field, in our circuses, vast numbers of innocent victims. By which pastimes the love of destruction of their own kind and all savage instincts have been strengthened, while at the same time the instincts of humanity and pity have been blunted and all but wholly extinguished.

The poet Cowper declared:

> I would not enter on my list of friends, though graced with polished manners and fine sense, yet wanting sensibility, the man who needlessly sets foot upon a worm.

Two centuries later, his namesake, John Cowper Powys, wrote:

> The value of man is in his human qualities, his conscience, his nobility and magnanimity of soul. Modern scientific men have deliberately placed themselves outside human conscience.

He was to be echoed by another novelist, Brigid Brophy, with 'the whole case for behaving decently to animals rests on the fact that we are the superior species'.

This is the complete answer to the man who, when you complain of his cruelty, will tell you that 'nature is cruel' or that 'a cat with a mouse is being cruel'.

Albert Schweitzer hopefully foresaw the day when 'public opinion will no longer tolerate *amusements* based on the mal-treatment and killing of animals'. We should like to think so too, but in spite of the abolition of bear-baiting and bull-baiting there is too much evidence to the contrary. We have progressed but little, when one considers that Montaigne in his great essay on cruelty could say 'For my own part I cannot without grief see so much as an innocent beast pursued and killed, that has no defence and from whom we have received no offence at all'.

Wild animals and birds, even in a 'civilized' society, lead lives of constant apprehension and terror. Long experience of man has taught them never to trust him, that he is always the enemy. Hardy bears this out in his ironic poem 'The Baby and the Wagtail'. The baby, exemplifying innocence, watches a ford where a wagtail is disporting itself. A bull, a stallion and a cur go through the ford but the bird is not frightened by any of them, although they are the fiercest of their kind. But on the appearance of a 'perfect gentleman' the bird 'In terror rose and disappeared—the baby fell a-thinking'. And so may we all. Walking on a lonely hill, the authors observed a pair of wild duck flying over on their way to a pool in the valley. They must have spotted the humans far beneath them, for they suddenly took alarm and wheeled to give us a wide berth. We had no guns and wished them no harm.

Often naturalists and humane members of the public try to succour some wounded animal or injured bird, always to be met with this deadly fear of human beings. Wild life cannot believe that we ever mean them any good, and unfortunately they have all too firm grounds for their suspicious and wary attitudes.

At Peter Scott's Wildfowl Trust, at Slimbridge in Gloucestershire, there is mounted a brief but telling exhibition illustrating man's achievements on both the creative and destructive level. On the one hand are pictures of artistic and and constructive achivements, on the other a few of his crimes against creation—Coventry in 1941, Hiroshima, the death camps. Between them the visitor faces a mirror and can read a description of our human race in the following caption:

Look into the frame below and you will see a specimen of the *most dangerous and destructive animal* the world has ever known.

# Bibliography

| | |
|---|---|
| BUXTON, Anthony | *Fisherman Naturalist* (Collins 1950) |
| BYRT, Mabel | *Call of the River* (Country Life 1956) |
| CARSON, Rachel | *Silent Spring* (Hamish Hamilton 1963) |
| CHRISTIAN, Garth | *While Some Trees Stand* (Newnes 1963) |
| CHURCHWARD, Capt. R. S. | *Master of Hounds Speaks* (NAACS 1951) |
| COUNCIL FOR NATURE | *British Predatory Mammals* (Zoological Society 1967) |
| DREYFUS, Marie | *Crimes Against Creation* (Massey & Co 1960) |
| FITTER, Richard | *Vanishing Wild Animals of the World* (Kaye & Ward & Midland Bank 1968) |
| HANSARD | from 1948 to 1969 |
| HARRIS, C. J. | *Otters* (Weidenfeld & Nicolson 1968) |
| HARRISON, Ruth | *Animal Machines* (V. Stuart 1964) |
| HARRISON MATTHEWS, L. | *Beasts of the Field* (Collins 1964) |
| HUXLEY, Elspeth | *Brave New Victuals* (Chatto & Windus 1965) |
| LANCUM, F. Howard | *Wild Animals and the Land* (HMSO 1948) |
| LEE, R. | *A Natural History* (Longmans 1844) |
| LEUTSCHER, Alfred | *Tracks and Signs British Mammals* (Macmillan 1960) |
| MARKS, John | *To the Bullfight again* (André Deutsch 1956) |
| MATHEISSEN, Peter | *Wild Life in America* (Viking Press 1966) |
| MAXWELL, Gavin | *Ring of Bright Water* (Longmans Green 1960) |
| MAXWELL, Gavin | *Raven Seek Thy Brother* (Longmans Green 1968) |
| MILNE, L. & M. | *Water and Life* (André Deutsch 1965) |
| MILNE, L. & M. | *The Senses of Animals and Men* (Atheneum, New York, 1964) |
| MOORE, Patrick (Ed) | *Against Hunting* (Gollancz 1965) |

| | |
|---|---|
| MORRIS, Desmond | *The Naked Ape* (Jonathan Cape 1968) |
| MOSS, A. (RSPCA) | *Valiant Crusade* (Cassell 1961) |
| MURRAY, Ruth | *Badgers* (David & Charles, to be published) |
| NEAL, Ernest | *The Badger* (Collins 1948) |
| PINE, Leslie | *After their Blood* (Kimber 1960) |
| PODHAISKY, Col. | *White Stallions of Vienna* (Harrap 1963) |
| RYDER, Vera | *Living With Monkeys* (Dent 1967) |
| SHUHMACHER, Eugen | *Last of the Wild* (Collins 1968) |
| TAYLOR PAGE, F. J. | *Field Guide British Deer* (Mammal Soc. 1957) |
| TURNER, E. S. | *All Heaven in a Rage* (Michael Joseph 1964) |
| WILLIAMSON, Henry | *Tales of a Devon Village* (Faber 1945) |
| WINDISCH-GRAETZ, Mathilde | *The Spanish Riding School* (Cassell 1960) |

# British Organisations, Humane and Welfare Societies, including Commonwealth

RSPCA,
105 Jermyn Street, London SW1

NATIONAL CANINE DEFENCE LEAGUE,
10 Seymour Street, London W1

NATIONAL COUNCIL FOR ANIMALS' WELFARE,
126 Royal College Street, London NW1

NATIONAL EQUINE DEFENCE LEAGUE,
Blackwell, Carlisle

NATIONAL SOCIETY FOR ABOLITION OF CRUEL SPORTS
7 Lloyd Square, London WC1

OUR DUMB FRIENDS' LEAGUE,
Grosvenor Gardens House, Victoria, London SW1

PEOPLE'S DISPENSARY FOR SICK ANIMALS,
PDSA House, Clifford Street, London W1

PERFORMING ANIMALS' DEFENCE LEAGUE,
11 Buckingham Street, London WC2

PROTECTION OF LIVESTOCK FOR SLAUGHTER ASSOCIATION,
30a Lawrence Road, Liverpool 15

ROYAL SOCIETY FOR THE PROTECTION OF BIRDS,
The Lodge, Sandy, Bedfordshire

ANGLO-EAST EUROPEAN FUND for Animal Welfare,
37a Smith Sreet, London SW3

SCOTTISH ANIMAL WELFARE,
6 Church Drive, Lenzie, Glasgow

SCOTTISH SPCA,
19 Melville Street, Edinburgh 3

COUNCIL OF JUSTICE TO ANIMALS AND HUMANE SLAUGHTER ASSOCIATION,
42 Old Bond Street, London W1

UFAW. (Universities Federation Animal Welfare),
230 High Street, Potters Bar, Herts.

DARTMOOR LIVESTOCK PRO-
TECTION SOCIETY,
Sanduck, Lustleigh, Newton
Abbot, Devon

ANIMAL DEFENCE and ANTI-
VIVISECTION SOCIETY,
15 St. James's Place, London
SW1

BEAUTY WITHOUT
CRUELTY,
The Lady Dowding, Oakgates,
Southborough, Tunbridge Wells,
Kent

BRITISH UNION FOR THE
ABOLITION OF VIVISECTION,
47 Whitehall, London SW1

CAPTIVE ANIMALS PROTEC-
TION SOCIETY,
Sec., Miss I. M. Heaton, 46
Pembroke Crescent, Hove 3,
Sussex

PERFORMING ANIMALS DE-
FENCE LEAGUE,
Castle Chambers, Torquay
Devon

CRUSADE AGAINST ALL
CRUELTY TO ANIMALS,
Avenue Lodge, Bounds Green
Road, London N22

GLASGOW AND WEST SCOT-
LAND SOCIETY FOR THE
PREVENTION OF CRUELTY
TO ANIMALS,
15 Royal Terrace, Glasgow, C3

INTERNATIONAL CULTURAL
FORUM, UK sponsoring The
International Animals' Charter,
127 Nevill Avenue, Hove 4,
Sussex

INTERNATIONAL LEAGUE
FOR THE PROTECTION OF
HORSES,
4 Bloomsbury Square, London
WC1

IRISH UNION FOR ABOLI-
TION OF VIVISECTION,
Sec., Miss Margaret Bassett, 17
Charleville Road, Rathmines,
Dublin

KINDNESS CLUB,
252 Waterloo Row, Fredericton,
New Brunswick, Canada

LEAGUE AGAINST CRUEL
SPORTS,
58 Maddox Street, London W1

REPUBLIC OF IRELAND,
IRISH LEAGUE AGAINST
CRUEL SPORTS,
Innisaimer, Dalkey Avenue,
Dalkey, Co. Dublin. Hon. Sec:
Mrs. H. Noble

SCOTTISH SOCIETY FOR
THE PREVENTION OF VIVI-
SECTION,
Sec: Mr. Harvey Metcalf, FCIS,
10 Queensberry Street, Edin-
burgh 2

ULSTER SOCIETY FOR THE
PREVENTION OF CRUELTY
TO ANIMALS,
16 Montgomey Street, Belfast

UNIVERSITIES FEDERATION
FOR ANIMAL WELFARE,
230 High Street, Potters Bar,
Herts.

WORLD LEAGUE AGAINST
VIVISECTION AND FOR THE
PROTECTION OF ANIMALS,
5 North View, Wimbledon,
London SW19

THE CANADIAN WILD HORSE
SOCIETY,
1120 Bird Road, Richmond BC

FAUNA PRESERVATION
SOCIETY,
c/o Zoological Society of London,
Regents Park, London NW1

THE FARM AND FOOD
SOCIETY,
37 Tanza Road, London NW3

THE NEW FOREST SOCIETY,
Palfreylands, Dibden Purlieu,
Southampton SO4 5Qa

NATIONAL ANTI-VIVISEC-
TION SOCIETY LTD.
51 Harley Street, Loudon W1

COMPASSION IN WORLD
FARMING,
Copse House, Greatham, Liss,
Hants.

BRITISH SOCIETY FOR
SOCIAL RESPONSIBILITY IN
SCIENCE,
42 Great Russell Street, London
WC1

CO-ORDINATING COMMIT-
TEE ON FACTORY FARMING,
Orwell, Buckbury Lane, New-
port, IOW

INTERNATIONAL COUNCIL
AGAINST BULL FIGHTING
10 Queensborough Terrace,
London W2

# RSPCA Branches Abroad

NIGERIA SPCA
Sec: 11 Grey Street, PO Box
104, Yaba, Nigeria

TANZANIA SPCA
Executive Director: PO Box 1844,
Dar es Salaam, Tanzania

PENANG STATE
Hon. Sec: PO Box 135, Penang,
Malaysia

CYPRUS SPCA
Nicosia: Chairman: 4 Acheon
Street, Nicosia, Cyprus
Limassol: Chairman: PO Box
34, Limassol, Cyprus

UGANDA SPCA
Hon. Sec: PO Box 3293, Kampala,
Uganda

GUYANA
Hon. Sec: Animal Clinic, Robb
Street and Orange Walk, George-
town, Demerara

SINGAPORE SPCA
Sec: Old Orchard Road, Post
Office, Singapore 9

MOMBASA AND DISTRICT
SPCA
Chairman: PO Box 379, Mom-
basa, Kenya

GIBRALTAR
Hon. Sec: RSPCA Clinic,
Cathedral Square, Gibraltar

SEYCHELLES
Hon. Sec: PO Box 32, Mahe,
Seychelles

MALTA
Hon. Sec: Dog's Home, Floriana,
Malta, GC

ANTIGUA
Sec: PO Box 215, St. John's,
Antigua, West Indies

GRENADA
Hon Sec: PO Box 156, St. George's
Grenada, BWI

BARBADOS
Sec: Cheltenham Lodge, Lands
End, Fontabelle, Barbados

LUANSHYA
Hon. Sec: PO Box 216, Luanshya,
Zambia

MULFULIRA
Hon. Sec: PO Box 712, Mulfulira,
Zambia

NCHANGA–CHINGOLA
Hon. Sec: PO Box 320, Chingola,
Zambia

ISLAND OF ST. HELENA
Hon. Sec: Jamestown, Island of
St. Helena, S. Atlantic Ocean

# List of Associated Sister Societies

ALDERNEY ANIMAL WEL-
FARE SOCIETY
Hon. Sec: St. Anne's Club, Val
Road, Alderney

BERMUDA SPCA
Sec: Animal Shelter, Valley Road,
Paget West, Bermuda

BULAWAYO SPCA
The Sec: PO Box 1321, Khani
Road, Bulawayo, R

CANADIAN COUNCIL FOR
ANIMALS' WELFARE
Nat. Sec: PO Box 75, Great
Village, Nova Scotia

CANADIAN FEDERATION OF
HUMANE SOCIETIES
Corres. Sec: 95 Bayview Road,
Ottawa 3, Ontario

CANADIAN SPCA
General Manager: 5215, Jean
Talon Street West, Montreal 9,
Canada

CAPE OF GOOD HOPE SPCA
Sec: Box 3, Plumstead, Cape
Town, South Africa

CEYLON DUMB FRIENDS
WELFARE ASSOCIATION
The Sec: 23 Hamers Avenue,
Colombo 6, Ceylon

DEESIDE ANIMAL WELFARE
SOCIETY
Hon. Sec: Stamford Bach, Holy-
well, Flints.

DEVONPORT (TASMANIA)
SPCA
Sec: GPO Box 180, Devonport,
Tasmania

TASMANIA SPCA (NORTHERN DIVISION)
Hon. Sec: 40 Salisbury Crescent, West Launceston, Tasmania

DURBAN AND COAST SPCA
The Sec: 83/5, Sydney Road, Durban, Natal

KENYA SPCA
Sec: PO Box 157, Nairobi, Kenya

EAST LONDON (SA) SPCA
Sec.-Treasurer: PO Box 282, East London, S. Africa

FIJI SPCA
Hon. Sec: 155 Queen's Road, Suva, Fiji

GUERNSEY SPCA
Hon Sec: Courtil Le Petit Clos, Route St. George, Catel, Guernsey

JAMAICA SPCA
Exec. Sec: 115 Spanish Town Road, Denham Town PO, Kingston, Jamaica

JERSEY SPCA
Hon. Sec: 89 St. Saviour's Road, St. Helier, Jersey

JOHANNESBURG SPCA
Sec: PO Box 2960, Ophir-Booysens Road, Booysens, Johannesburg

KARACHI SPCA
Corres. to Mrs. A. N. Fatakia, 36 Fifth East Street, PDSOCHS, Karachi 4 W Pakistan

KOBE (JAPAN) SPCA
Sec: c/o Oppenheimer & Cie Ltd., 35 Nishi-Machi, Ikuta-ku, Kobe (PO Box 93)

MALLORCA SPCA
Mrs. Reynolds, La Turquesa, Paguera, Mallorca

MANX SPCA
Hon. Sec: "Trelja", Selborne Drive, Douglas, IOM

MAURITIUS SPCA
Hon Sec: Reduit, Colony of Mauritius, Indian Ocean

NDOLA SPCA
Sec: PO Box 2142, Ndola, Zambia

ONTARIO HUMANE SOCIETY
Gen. Man: 696 Yonge Street, Toronto 5, Ontario

OSLO SPCA
Sec: Foreningen Til Dyrenes Beskyttelse, Karl Johans Gate, 12b Oslo, Norway

PAPUA AND NEW GUINEA SPCA
Vice-President: POB 531 Port Moresby, Papua

PHILIPPINE ANIMAL WELFARE SOCIETY
Sec: PO Box 3279, Manila, PI

PIETERMARITZBURG SPCA
Sec: 178a Longmarket Street, Pietermaritzburg, Natal, SA

PORT ELIZABETH SPCA
Sec: PO Box 7036, 7th Milestone, Cape Road, Port Elizabeth, SA

RSPCA NEW SOUTH WALES
Sec: 15 Randle Street, Sydney, NSW, Australia

RSPCA (VICTORIA)
Sec: 112 Wellington Parade, Melbourne, Australia

ROYAL FEDERATION OF NEW ZEALAND S'sPCA Inc.
Sec: PO Box 388, Blenheim, New Zealand

ROYAL QUEENSLAND SOCIETY FOR PREVENTION OF CRUELTY
Sec: 301 Fairfield Road, Fairfield, Brisbane, Australia

SOCIEDADE PROTECTORA DOS ANIMALS
Rua de Sao Paulo 55, 2 Dt, Lisbon, Portugal

SOCIETY FOR THE PROTECTION OF ANIMALS IN N. AFRICA
Organiser: 15 Buckingham Gate, London SW1

SOCIETE POUR LA DEFENSE DES ANIMAUX
Hon. Sec: Mrs. M. de Sivers, 38 Bis, Avenue Marechal Joffre, Nice, AM

SOUTH AFRICAN FEDERATION OF S'sPCA
Sec: 437 Edmund Street, Arcadia, Pretoria

SPCA AUSTRALIAN CAPITAL TERRITORY
Hon. Sec: PO Box 23, O'Connor, Canberra, ACT

SOUTH AUSTRALIA RSPCA
Sec: 7 Greenhill Road, Adelaide, Australia

SPCA SALISBURY
Sec: PO Box 177, Salisbury, Rhodesia

SWAZILAND SPCA
Hon. Sec: PO Box 501, Mbabane, Swaziland, South Africa

TRINIDAD AND TOBAGO SPCA
Sec: PO Box 954, 189a Tracarete Road, Port of Spain, Trinidad, BWI

ULSTER SPCA
Org. Sec: Miss N. Parker, 65 May Street, Belfast, N. Ireland

WAIKATO (NZ) SPCA
Hon. Sec: 96 Galloway Street, Hamilton East, New Zealand

WESTERN AUSTRALIA RSPCA
Gen. Sec: Occidental House, St. George's Terrace, Perth, W. Australia

# Index

187

cruelty of, 40–1
cult of, 42–3
history of, 35
romance of, 34
tourist influence on, 42–3
bulls, 32, 36–7, 40–2, 44–6
Burden, Frederick, MP, 89, 102, 104
Burns, M., 62
Burns, Robert, 11

cages, 62–3, 65–6
Calvert, Albert F., 37
camels, 134–5
Canada, 56, 114, 121–5, 143–4, 168–169, 172
Canadian SPCA, 114, 122
Canadian Wild Horse Society, 56
Captive Animals Protection Society, 32
captive bolt pistols, 108–9
Carding, Jane, 155
Carson, Rachel, 100–1, 163–5
Catholic Study Circle for Animal Welfare, 66, 173–4
cats
  Civet cats, 32
  domestic cats, 60–1, 174
  experiments on, 152
cattle, 94–8, 100, 104–8, 132
Cavalini's Dogs, 21
Chalmers Mitchell, Sir Peter, 28
chemical sprays, 162–9
Cherrington, John, 98, 100
children
  at bullfights, 40, 44
  at circuses, 22, 28–9, 31, 33
  cruelty of, 174–5
  at hunts, 69, 72, 76, 92
  at slaughterhouses, 109
chimpanzees, 20–1, 30, 67
chinchilla, 127
Chipperfield, 32
Christian, Garth, 85
Churchward, Captain Robert, 76
Cintrón, Conchita, 45–6
circuses
  appeal to cruelty, 24
  children at, 22, 28–9, 31, 33
  decline in popularity, 32–3

legislation attempts, 28–30
relations with RSPCA, 18
winter quarters, 16–17
*see also* names of individual circuses
*City of Waterford*, 118–19
civets, 127
Coakes, Marion, 54
Conibear, Frank, 120
Cook, Thomas, 35, 37, 40
Court, Alfred, 24–6
Crouch, Robert, MP, 110
Crusade Against All Animal Cruelty, 108
curare, 129

*Daily Mail*, 24, 54–5, 126
Daily Telegraph, 64, 101, 105
Dartmoor Livestock Protection Society, 115–16
Davies, Brian, 143
Davy, John, 129
DDT *see* chemical sprays
deer, 73, 77–8, 80, 150
Denmark, 30, 60, 172
de Rivera, Primo, 39
dogs
  experiments on, 145–7, 152–8
  for hunting, 69–92
  overbreeding of, 62
  performing dogs, 21–2
  stray dogs, 59–61, 172
Domecq, Don Pedro, 36
donkeys, 132–8, 140
Dowding, Air Chief Marshal, Lord, 127
draught animals, 130ff.
drugs, 106, 148–9
Dugdale, J. MP, 99, 104
Durrell, Gerald, 65

Eastern Europe, 131
*Economist*, 102
Edgar, Frederick, 51
Egypt, 134–9
Eire, 60, 119
El Cordobes, 35, 42–3
'Elephant Bill', 27
elephants, 15, 17, 26–7, 32